BEGINNING
PHILOSOPHIC

Roger Simonds
American University

University Press
of America™

958766

To the memory of

Elsie H. Simonds

who taught the deaf
and the blind

"To open the blind eyes,
to bring out the prisoners from the prison,
and them that sit in darkness
out of the prison house."
(Isaiah 42:7)

PREFACE

Authors of new logic books customarily begin by offering an apology for introducing still another text into an already crowded market. This book needs no apology of that sort, because it is different. First, it deals with philosophy as well as logic, and at the present writing there are only three other American texts which make any serious attempt to combine these topics. Secondly, it is a philosophical logic for beginners, suitable for a one-semester introductory course in logic.

For many students, an introductory logic course may be the only exposure to philosophy they get. Within these limits, one cannot expect to penetrate very far into the mysteries of logical theory or the puzzlements of philosophy. But one can expect to gain some insight into the fact that logical theory is an important branch of philosophy which, in a certain sense, takes precedence over all the others; for all systematic theorizing depends on the patterns of valid reasoning that are investigated in logical theory. A person who has acquired this insight need not be afraid to explore the reputedly dangerous labyrith of philosophical thought. He has the thread that will guide him through it.

The logic developed in this book is largely the traditional "Aristotelian" system which was taken for granted by Western philosophers from ancient times down to the end of the nineteenth century. This system provided much of the terminology and subject-matter for the classics of our philosophical tradition. Its principles have guided and constrained speculation, and never more firmly than when the philosophers themselves were unconscious of their presence. Descartes, the "father of modern philosophy", was so little concerned with questions of logical theory that he was willing to hand over the teaching of that subject to the rhetoricians. The result of this was not that the traditional principles of logic had no effect in his philosophy but rather that their operation was unperceived. Even Kant, who thought of himself as a philosophical revolutionary, incorporated the traditional logic into his system and explicitly declared it to be perfect and complete. Non-Aristotelian logic, like non-Euclidean geometry, is a very recent development, and its influence is only just beginning to be felt. Contemporary students need to become aware of the shortcomings of traditional logic, in order to understand these recent developments; but first they must have a good grasp of the traditional concepts and of their more salient effects in philosophy.

With these ideas in mind, I have departed from the conventional choice and ordering of topics in several ways. Singular propositions are given more prominence here than in any other text, because I regard the theory of singulars as the real but neglected starting point of traditional logical theory, as it was in Aristotle's Organon, and because it is one of the main connecting links between logical theory and other aspects of philosophy. For similar reasons, I introduce modal concepts at an early stage and develop some basic features of their philosophical use. Most introductory texts do not deal with these concepts at all. The traditional rules of inference are not only presented (chapters 4 through 6) but are also explained and justified much more fully than usual. Some devices found in most texts, such as Venn diagrams, have been deliberately omitted because they foster confusion betweendifferent orientations, or because they make unneccessary complications. On the other hand, the "distribution shorthand" given here, which greatly simplifies the analysis of traditional patterns of inference, is not found elsewhere. The problem of "existential import" receives much more thorough treatment than usual; and the problem of non-existent individuals is also discussed, leading to an informal presentation of Russell's theory of descriptions (not usually mentioned in elementary texts). The last chapter offers a few glimpses into the wider world of modern logical theory.

The exercises provided at the end of most sections of the text should be worked out carefully for the sake of comprehension, and they can be used as a focus for class discussion. The instructor will probably want to supplement the material of this book, as the writer himself does, by assigning other readings on philosophy, on inductive reasoning and scientific method, or perhaps on rhetoric.

The American University
June, 1977

TABLE OF CONTENTS

I. LOGIC AND PHILOSOPHY

1. Why Study Logic?

Logic is generally defined as the art or science of reasoning. Hence it is obvious that anyone who is interested in the art or science of reasoning has, or should have, some interest in the study of logic. But it is not so obvious just what sort of interest is involved or just what benefits may be expected from the study of logic. Let us begin by clearing away some possible misconceptions.

First, if we think of logic as the "art" of reasoning, and if we think of the art of something as the skill or technique of doing it, then it seems natural to think that in learning logic we shall be learning how to reason. To some extent this may be true. For example, we can learn how to distinguish and evaluate various forms of argument or inference in ways that would probably not occur to us until we have studied the subject systematically. But the more complicated forms of reasoning that belong to the traditional subject-matter of logic are all derived from a very small number of elementary forms which we all use instinctively and continually. Logical theory does not justify or demonstrate these elementary forms; it simply takes them for granted. Given the information that

Water is wet,

plus the further information that

Violets are blue,

we can and do immediately draw the conclusion that

Water is wet, and violets are blue

without having had the benefit of a course in logic. Moreover, a little reflection shows that logical theory cannot justify every kind of reasoning; it must take some kinds of reasoning for granted in order to justify others, or else the "justification" will be circular. A person who did not know how to employ the elementary forms of reasoning would not find out how to do so from a logic-book, and he would not be able to follow the arguments in the book or understand what it was about.

Secondly, if we think of logic as the art of reasoning, and if we think of reasoning mainly as a means of persuasion, it may occur to us that the study of logic will be useful as a means of improving our debating skills. This idea is not altogether wrong, but it would be a mistake to expect very much from logic for this purpose. It is a great advantage in debate, of course, to be able to accuse your opponent of various logical fallacies, especially if you can give their names, and still better their classical Latin names (his argument is a non-sequitur; he has committed an ignoratio elenchi, a petitio principii, and so forth). But this tactic may be just as effective when he has not committed a fallacy as when he has, if the audience is willing to believe you. On the other hand, you may find the audience unwilling to accept your conclusion even when your facts are solidly established and your argument logically unassailable. Since the problem of persuasion is a psychological problem, knowledge of logical theory is not sufficient to deal with it; and for purposes of persuasion it is often more important to seem logical than to be logical. There are many successful debaters who know little or nothing about logical theory, and there are many expert logicians who have little skill in debate.

Thirdly, if we think of logic as the "science" of reasoning, we may perhaps think of it as describing the patterns of reasoning that people actually use or have used in the past. This point of view would give logic the status of a social science, like anthropology. Accordingly, one might expect the logician to compare the typical patterns of reasoning that occur in the Occident with those that occur in the Orient or in primitive cultures. Or one might expect him to be an historian of the development of patterns of reasoning in the literature of some particular culture. Certainly there is a place for studies of this kind, and to some degree they are of interest to any student of logic; but they are not the main focus of attention in logical theory. Logical theory is concerned with what is correct or incorrect, sound or unsound, valid or fallacious in reasoning. In this sense logic is a prescriptive or normative science rather than a descriptive science. It has more in common with, say, ethics and jurisprudence than with history and sociology. Now there will always be some people -- skeptics and relativists -- who will tell you that nothing is really either good or bad, right or wrong, correct or incorrect, but thinking makes it so; and thinking, they will say, is controlled unconsciously by the values or prejudices instilled in us by the cultural environment in which we were born and raised. This point of view has its attractions, at first, for those who feel exhilarated at the idea of being free to think what they please without being fettered by rules. But the exhilaration fades somewhat when one sees that the fetters of "unconscious cultural bias" are at least equally confining. Moreover, there is no way to take the doctrines of skepticism and relativism seriously without subverting them in the process. A man who argues that there is no difference between good and bad reasoning is a man who tacitly takes for granted the truth of what he ostensibly denies. The same can be said of a man who draws conclusions from such a position. On the other hand, this man may not be willing to abandon his position merely because these facts have been pointed out to him; logic has no magical power to persuade.

What then is the main benefit to be expected from the study of logic? It is not the acquisition of a skill, nor is it a knowledge of facts. It is insight that we are after: a better understanding of the workings of our own mind and the relations of ideas. This insight is completely general, since it is not confined to any particular set of ideas or subject-matter; every kind of intellectual activity makes use of it. This insight is also completely independent, since it requires or presupposes nothing other than itself; we do not need to acquire some knowledge or skill in order to have it, but we need only let it develop by paying attention to its presence. For these reasons there are some very intimate connections between the study of logic and the study of philosophy, as we shall see.

2. Validity, Soundness and Fallacies

Reasoning is a process of thought in which we pass from one thought or idea to another, but it is more than a mere passage. I may pass from the thought that something is a square to the thought that it is a rectangle, without reasoning, simply by having first the one thought and then the other. This might be called "free association." In this example, of course, it is obvious that the second thought follows logically from the first: if something is a square, then it must be a rectangle. But I was not necessarily aware of

- 3 -

that fact in passing from one thought to the other. In reasoning, I do not merely think that something is true; I think that it is true because something else is true. I am drawing a conclusion, making an inference. The inference is that special kind of passage from thought to thought that represents my awareness or belief that the truth of the second thought is guaranteed by the truth of the first; the conclusion is the end result of the inference. The thought or thoughts from which the conclusion is drawn are the premises of the inference (often also called 'assumptions' or 'hypotheses'). Thus I might draw the conclusion

This is a rectangle

from the single premise

This is a square,

or I might draw the same conclusion from the pair of premises

This is a square

and

All squares are rectangles.

An inference may or may not be expressed in language; we may express premises or conclusions, or both, without expressing the inference itself. Reasoning which is expressed in language is called argument. Practically, it is obvious that we can deal with reasoning only by dealing with arguments, which are open to public inspection and analysis.

An argument is valid if and only if the truth of its premises guarantees the truth of its conclusion. To say that the truth of the premises (P) guarantees the truth of the conclusion (C) is to say that it is not possible for P to be true without C also being true; in other words, it is necessarily the case if P is true then C is true.

A valid argument, however, does not always have a true conclusion, because its premise may in fact be false. Thus on the premise that

The District of Columbia has a square shape

it is quite proper to conclude that

    The District of Columbia is rectangular,

although in fact the District of Columbia is bounded
on the West by the irregular contours of the Potomac
River and is not square at all. A valid argument may
have a true conclusion, moreover, without having true
premises. Thus we can arrive validly at the true conclusion that

    Harvard is a university

from the premises that

    Harvard is a public secondary school

and

    All public secondary schools are universities,

both of which are obviously false. In these ways, the
truth-value (truth or untruth) of premises and conclusions is independent of the validity or invalidity
of arguments. It is not completely independent, however, because a valid argument cannot have true premises with a false conclusion.

    An argument is sound if and only if it is valid
and has true premises. Thus every sound argument is
valid, but not every valid argument is sound. And
every sound argument has a true conclusion, since it
has true premises which guarantee the truth of its
conclusion. But an argument with a true conclusion
is not necessarily sound, even if it happens to be
valid, since it may also happen to have false premises.
Although there is only one way for an argument to be
sound, namely by being

    valid with true premises,

there are three ways for an argument to be unsound,
namely by being

    valid with false premises,

    invalid with true premises, or

    invalid with false premises.

Clearly only a sound argument can be relied upon to produce a true conclusion, and in any of the three types of unsound argument the conclusion may turn out to be false.

Traditionally, unsound arguments are called 'fallacies', and if they are unsound by being invalid they are called 'formal fallacies'. The reason for this terminology is that the rules governing validity in arguments are formal rules; an argument is valid or invalid by virtue of its form or type, without regard (in a certain sense) to the actual content of the premises and conclusions. But the sense in which this is the case can only be understood by examining the various kinds of elementary forms of argument. Fallacies other than formal fallacies have usually been called 'informal fallacies' or 'material fallacies', and one might expect these to be valid arguments with false premises; but in fact there does not seem to be any well-established standard use for these terms, and we shall not need them in this book.

It is important to realize -- and this may come as a shock to the beginner -- that many of the arguments actually used in every-day speaking and writing, perhaps even most of them, are technically unsound. And nevertheless they are often accepted with equanimity, even by people who are fully aware of their being unsound. The reason is that arguments are only rarely stated in full; they are made explicit, as a rule, only to the extent that seems necessary in order to gain agreement. We do not like to belabor the obvious. Very frequently, one or more of the premises that would be needed to justify a conclusion are omitted, if it seems likely that the listener will supply them for himself without hesitation, or if the speaker does not want to draw attention to them. Often the premises are given, but not the conclusion, if the speaker wants the listener to reach the conclusion (probably a very obvious one) by himself. Arguments of this kind, with one or more missing parts, are called <u>enthymemes</u>. They are among the most useful items in the rhetorician's bag of tricks. One does not often see arguments like

Socrates is a man, and all men are mortal; so Socrates is mortal.

But one does frequently see arguments like

Socrates is a man, so Socrates is mortal

- 6 -

or

        All men are mortal, so Socrates is mortal

or

        Socrates is a man, and all men are mortal,

where there is little doubt that the listener or reader
will supply the missing premise or conclusion and
accept the result as a valid argument. We never accuse
a man of reasoning illogically merely because he has
offered an enthymeme; if we want to reject his conclusion, we usually accuse him of tacitly assuming a false
premise. In fact, we go to some lengths to avoid the
accusation of irrationality. If a man tells us that

        Water is wet, because $2 + 2 = 4$,

we would rather believe that he is joking, or that he
is using the word 'because' in some peculiar sense, if
it seems improbable that he is actually entertaining
some tacit premise to the effect that

        If $2 + 2 = 4$, then water is wet,

which would transform the enthymeme into a valid
argument.

        Since any enthymeme can be transformed into a
valid argument by adding appropriate premises or conclusion, the study of enthymemes is not of interest in
logical theory; but the art of recognizing missing premises or conclusions is very important in the analysis
of actual arguments, and this art depends on a knowledge of the elementary argument-forms in logical theory.

                    EXERCISES

Decide if possible whether the following arguments are
sound or unsound. If unsound, do they fail to be valid,
or fail to have true premises, or both?

    1. Boston is the capital of Massachusetts, and
        Boston is a seaport; therefore, the capital
        of Massachusetts is a seaport.

    2. Boston is the capital of New Jersey, and
        Boston is a seaport; therefore, the capital
        of New Jersey is a seaport.

3. Boston is the capital of Massachusetts, and
    Boston is a seaport; therefore, the capital
    of Massachusetts is not a seaport.

4. Washington is the capital of Massachusetts,
    and Washington is not a seaport; therefore,
    the capital of Massachusetts is a seaport.

5. The Devil is an ingenious fellow, and all
    ingenious fellows are clever; therefore,
    the Devil is clever.

3. Logic in Philosophy

In the original and widest sense, according to
the Oxford English Dictionary, philosophy is the
"love, study, or pursuit of wisdom, or of knowledge
of things and their causes, whether theoretical or
practical." This is the classical conception of
philosophy in Western civilization, as one can see
by examining the enormous range of interests and
topics in the writings of the classical Greek philosophers. Today it would be almost unthinkable for a
philosopher to attempt to work effectively in all of
the different fields of study covered by Aristotle,
for instance: logic, rhetoric, literary and dramatic
criticism, physical science, biology, psychology,
ethics, political theory, metaphysics, theology.
Merely by naming the titles of Aristotle's works, one
begins to realize how much of what he considered philosophy would today be assigned to some special science
or discipline.

The tendency of philosophy to break up into parts,
creating new sciences which live separate lives, has
prompted pessimists to suggest that before long there
will be nothing left for philosophers to do. This
suggestion is based on two misconceptions. In the first
place, the various separate sciences are not really as
independent as college catalogs make them look. Physics,
chemistry, astronomy, the earth sciences, and the life
sciences, for example, all share certain general ideas
and methods in common; they could not have developed
successfully in isolation from each other. The modern
conception of scientific method, in particular, is
philosophical in origin and in character. In the second
place, every special science or discipline restricts its
range of interest to certain types of problems or to the
investigation of certain kinds of phenomena, without
which it would not be "special". But philosophy is
completely general in principle; it does not limit its

range of interest to any special class of questions. Thus there is really no basis for the fear that the subject-matter of philosophy will some day be completely absorbed by the special sciences. On the contrary, the more special sciences are created, the more pressing becomes the problem of integrating or harmonizing the various sciences with each other so as to obtain a consistent and adequate understanding of the world. And this is a philosophical problem.

Since there is no way to arrive at a consistent and adequate understanding of the world without reasoning, it is clear that logic must be an indispensable instrument for the philosopher. In this sense, the relationship of logic to philosophy is like that of mathematics to the physical sciences. But the relationship is also much more intimate. Logic is part and parcel of philosophy, not just an instrument for it, while mathematics is not part of the physical sciences. A physicist must make use of the laws of arithmetic, for example, in developing his theories and designing experiments; but the laws of arithmetic are quite independent of physical theory and not considered to be part of it. But philosophy, being completely general, excludes nothing from its subject-matter. Hence even logic itself is part of that subject-matter. Does this mean that the philosopher is free to construct or manipulate the laws of reasoning to suit the demands of his own philosophical system of ideas? Not at all. Philosophers take for granted the elementary forms of argument, just as everyone else does, whether consciously or unconsciously. These elementary forms, and the way in which we understand and apply them, have a decisive effect on the development of philosophical systems.

The philosopher's task may be put most simply in terms of the general question:

What is true?

But as soon as one considers this question, one sees also that the answer to it is not obvious, and some systematic method for attacking it is urgently needed. Hence one goes on to ask,

How, or to what extent, can we find out what is true?

At this point, logical theory has an important contribution to make, since it shows us in general what must be true _if_ various kinds of assumptions or premises are true; but it does not show in general how to choose the right premises.

A second contribution from logic, closely related to the first, is that it offers the philosopher a technical vocabulary and an algorism, or calculus, for the development of his ideas. The logical consequences of our ideas can emerge only when we have put those ideas in certain forms to which our basic patterns of logical inference can be applied. Thus even though logic does not determine the content of our ideas, it does limit the range of alternatives open to us. To a large extent, these limitations are built into the grammar of our language. In this way they are practically inescapable; or rather, they can be escaped only through the creation of new or artificial languages which may represent our logical and philosophical insights more adequately. Modern logical theory, over the past century, has developed many new forms of symbolism and new proof-procedures for this purpose. The influence of these developments on philosophy will be as profound as the influence of the discoveries of algebra, analytic geometry and the differential calculus on physical theory, although at present it is only just beginning to be felt.

At the end of this book, some of these new developments will be explored. Our main task, however, will be to understand the theory of logic in its traditional "Aristotelian" form, the form in which it governed the patterns of Western philosophical thought from classical times down to the end of the nineteenth century. Only by mastering this traditional theory and seeing its limitations can one understand why the technical innovations of modern logic are possible and useful.

II. SINGULAR PROPOSTIONS, INDIVIDUALS AND ATTRIBUTES

1. The Linguistic Framework

The traditions of Western logic and philosophy were established largely by men who thought, spoke and wrote in European languages. All of these languages, with only four exceptions,* belong to the Indo-European group of languages and have many common features which have influenced Western thought and culture. Most important for our purposes is their characteristic sentence-structure.

A sentence is what expresses a complete thought, and in all Indo-European languages a complete sentence must contain two basic elements: a subject and a predicate (or verb). In some languages both elements may be present in a single word. In Latin, for example, we have a complete sentence in the word

cogito

where the root-form 'cogit-' (from cogitare, to think) functions as predicate and the inflection '-o' (first person singular) functions as subject. In English, of course, we need at least two words:

I   think

(subject) (predicate)

although in every-day conversation one of these elements may be omitted. Thus in response to the question

What are you doing?

I may simply say

Thinking.

And in response to the question

Who is thinking?

---

*Finnish, Estonian, Hungarian and Basque.

I might say

> Me.

But these responses are understood as sentence-fragments rather than sentences, and the listener supplies the missing subject or predicate for himself.

Often the subject is a phrase instead of a single word:

> The reader of this book thinks.
>
> '------(subject)------' (predicate)

Or the predicate is a phrase:

> Aristotle wrote the first text-book on logic.
>
> (subject) '---------(predicate)-------------'

Or both:

> The man who discovered America was an Italian.
>
> '--------(subject)-----------' '--(predicate)-'

A sentence which contains other sentences as parts (sub-sentences) may be either a "compound" sentence, e.g.,

> There are black marbles in the box, but there are white ones too,

which consists entirely of two independent sub-sentences, or it may be a "complex" sentence, e.g.,

> The Egyptians, who were very clever, built pryamids.
>
> '--(sub-sentence)---'

A complex sentence has one or more subordinate sentences or clauses which function as parts of speech (noun, adjective, adverb). In the sample just mentioned, the sub-sentence 'who were very clever' functions as an adjective modifying the noun 'Egyptians'. In the sentence,

> Since he is poor, he pays no taxes,

the sub-sentence 'he is poor' functions as an adverb modifying the adjective 'no'.

The following is also a complex sentence:

Seneca said that man is a rational animal.

'-----(sub-sentence)----'

But this is not a complex sentence:

Seneca said, "Man is a rational animal."

because it does not contain a sub-sentence but only the name of such a sentence. A sentence which contains no sub-sentence is a "simple" sentence. Simple sentences have usually been thought more basic in that they are the "atoms" from which "molecular" compound or complex units of discourse are built up.

Indicative sentences, like

He closed the book

have been specially important for logic and philosophy because only they, as opposed to imperatives

Close the book!

or interrogatives

Did he close the book?

seem capable of being true or false. These differences of mood are not so fundamental as they look, however, since we could quite easily rewrite the above non-indicative examples in an indicative form, such as

I hereby command you to close the book

and

I want you to tell me whether he closed the book

without any important change of meaning. Construed in this way, interrogatives and imperatives are only abbreviations for relatively long-winded indicatives and are therefore just as capable of being true or false. If we do not normally think of them this way, it may be because we are not normally interested in their truth or untruth; ordinarily we just take their truth for granted. But if someone says

        Go jump over the moon

or

        Why are you such a blockhead?

we know that the speaker does not really want us to
do or say the things ostensibly called for.

        Whatever is true or false is said to have a
"truth-value" and is traditionally called a proposition.
Thus every true sentence is a proposition, and every
false (or untrue) sentence is a proposition.

        Sometimes it is argued that sentences cannot really
be propositions because different occurrences or
utterances of the same sentence may have different
meanings, or because different sentences may mean the
same thing. According to this view, the meanings of
sentences are propositions, not the sentences themselves.
For example, the sentence

        I am a student

seems to have different meanings according to who the
speaker is and when he is speaking. And on the other
hand

        Every tomato is red

seems to mean pretty much the same thing as

        Each tomato is red

or

        All tomatoes are red

or

        Any tomato is red

although these four sentences are obviously all different. Thus it seems quite plausible to argue that while
it is true or false that I am a student, the sentence
'I am a student' is not literally true or false but is
rather, say, correctly or incorrectly used on a given
occasion. The issue is more complicated and difficult
than it appears at first signt. Fortunately, we do not
have to resolve it for purposes of basic logical theory
or practice. Logical theory can deal with propositions

only by way of the expressions representing them in some language or other, and we can assume that these expressions -- i.e., sentences -- are propositions themselves, without running into any practical difficulties. That assumption will be made henceforth in this book.

We do not assume that all indicative sentences are propositions, for reasons to appear later. Among those sentences which we shall regard as propositions, some are simple sentences (containing no sub-sentences), and these are traditionally called <u>categorical propositions</u>. Among categorical propositions, we can distinguish those which have singular subjects and verb-forms, e.g.,

Paper burns

from those with plural forms, e.g.,

Papers burn.

The singular forms are used for two quite different purposes. A singular noun or subject-phrase may function as a common name, i.e., a name for a class or set of things. In the first of the two examples above, 'paper' clearly functions as a common name (or common noun). Or a singular subject may function as a proper name, i.e., a name for some particular individual person or things, as in

Plato wrote dialogues.

Since there is no purely formal indication of the difference between common names and proper names, we have to depend on our knowledge of the vocabulary of the language and on the general context. Nouns used as proper names (i.e., proper nouns) are usually capitalized, of course, but that is no help when they appear at the beginning of a sentence. Often we use a descriptive phrase instead of a proper noun, as in

The author of <u>War and Peace</u> was Russian,

where the subject-phrase, "The author of <u>War and Peace</u>', functions as a name for a particular individual. A descriptive phrase used in this way is called a "definite description". Note, however, that descriptive phrases are not always definite descriptions. For example, in

The wealthy householder is careful to lock his doors

'The wealthy householder' functions as a common name, not as a definite description.

Categorical propositions with singular subject-terms -- proper nouns or definite descriptions -- are traditionally known as <u>singular propositions</u>. All other categorical propositions are "quantified" propositions and are regarded as built up out of singulars in a manner to be investigated later.

It was a serious weakness in traditional logic that it did not possess any purely formal definition for the crucial concept of a singular proposition. As matters stand, there is no way to tell whether or not a proposition is "singular" without considering its meaning, and this is a most undesirable situation because of the vagueness and uncertainty thereby introduced into basic logical operations. Nevertheless, the notion of the singular proposition is so important that one can say without exaggeration that it is one of the central ideas in the Western philosophical tradition. It is a central idea in the writings of Aristotle, where much of the terminology, methods and principles of Western logic and philosophy were first clearly laid down. We explore this topic further in the next section.

EXERCISES

Compose your own illustrations of the following:

1. A simple sentence

2. A compound sentence

3. A complex sentence

4. A singular proposition with a proper noun as subject

5. A singular proposition with a definite description as subject.

6. A sentence with a common noun as subject

7. A sentence with a descriptive phrase, used as a common name, as subject.

2. The Correspondence-thesis

The reason why the notion of the singular proposition was so important in traditional philosophy is
that it was used to define the concept of reality, the
elements of the real world and the general form of
their relatedness. As a general principle, it was
assumed that a proposition is true if and only if
there is some corresponding situation or state of
affairs "in reality". Thus

The Taj Mahal is located in India

is a true proposition if and only if, in reality, the
Taj Mahal is located in India.

This general principle is what we shall call "the
correspondence-thesis". If we assume this principle,
and if we also make the traditional assumption that
the fundamental form of proposition is the singular
form, then in effect we have decided what the fundamental form of any real situation or state of affairs
must be. For we know that some real situation corresponds to every true singular proposition; but we also
know that some individual person or thing corresponds
to the subject-term of such a proposition (by definition, since it must be a proper name). Hence that
individual must be an element in the situation just as
its name, the subject-term, is an element in the
proposition. The other elements in the situation --
what remains when we disregard the individual mentioned
by the subject-term -- must correspond to the other
elements in the proposition. Assuming, of course, that
the proposition is true.

There are really three distinct elements involved
in a singular proposition: (1) its subject-term (a
proper noun or definite description), (2) its predicate-term (a verb or predicate phrase), and (3) the
implicit relationship (called "predication") between
these terms, which consists in the fact that when put
together in a certain order, or with certain grammatical signs, they form a complete sentence. Notice that
if we overlook this third factor, predication, we shall
be unable to distinguish, say,

Papers burn

from

Burn papers,

which are obviously different sentences, although the difference lies only in the word-order.

If the proposition that

Julius Caesar conquered Gaul

is true, as historians tell us, then there must be some real situation (by the correspondence-thesis) consisting of the fact that Julius Caesar conquered Gaul (or Julius Caesar's having conquered Gaul). There must be some such individual as Julius Caesar in reality, i.e., as an historical rather than fictional person, corresponding to the name 'Julius Caesar'. And there must be other elements of reality corresponding to the predicate and the relation of predication in the proposition. What corresponds to the predicate ('...conquered Gaul') is the attribute of having conquered Gaul. What corresponds to the relation of predication is a relation of attribution, whereby Julius Cassar "has" the attribute of having conquered Gaul.

Now consider the proposition that

Julius Caesar was the first President of the United States.

Since this is a false proposition, we do not assume that there is in reality any such thing as Julius Caesar's having been the first President of the United States, even though there was a Julius Caesar and there was a first President of the United States. In this case the correspondence fails because there is nothing to correspond to the relation of predication. In the case of

The Easter Bunny conquered Gaul

there is nothing to correspond to 'The Easter Bunny', so that traditionally one would not even grant this sentence the status of being a singular proposition. In the case of

Julius Caesar accomplished the impossible

we might argue that there really could be no such attribute as the attribute of having accomplished the impossible, which would raise a nice philosophical question. But in any case we can avoid this question by simply relying on the fact that, even if there were such an attribute in some sense, Julius Caesar could not have it.

The general idea of the correspondence-thesis can
be visualized in the following way:

Singular
  proposition: [Name--(associated by predication
                                    with)   --Predicate⌐
                                                           ⌐

Real
  Situation: [Individual -(associated by
                       attribution with) --Attribute]

The proposition is true if and only if all of the
correspondences, indicated by the vertical arrows, hold.
One might suppose, off hand, that a true proposition
might correspond to more than one real situation, or
that a real situation might correspond to more than one
true proposition. But on second thought one sees that
any difference between two situations, however slight,
can be formulated in different propositions if it can
be specified at all; and any difference between true
propositions if it amounts to anything more than a tri-
vial substitution of synonymous terms, must reflect some
difference in reality.

What we are calling an "individual", Aristotle
called a "primary substance". He also distinguished
nine general types of attributes (quantity, quality,
relation, place, time, position, state, action, affec-
tion) that might be assigned to a substance by a proposition. Thus he obtained ten general "categories" or
kinds of things corresponding to the ten different
kinds of names or phrases that he found in language.
How Aristotle arrived at these particular results need
not concern us; and in fact nobody knows quite how.
The important point to notice is that the correspondence-
thesis can be used, as Aristotle implicitly used it, to
define the notion of "the real world" (or reality, being,
actuality, existence). In this way it provides a
starting point for philosophy by way of a general definition of the "subject-matter" of philosophical thought.
What is the case in reality is defined as being what true
propositions describe.

One could use the correspondence-thesis in the
opposite way, too, that is, as a way to define 'truth'
in terms of "reality". When used in this way, the
thesis is usually called "the correspondence theory of
truth". This approach is less promising, however, because it assumes that we have some previously established
notions of reality and its elements. Those notions

are abstract and unclear in comparison to the less pretentious notions of language, sentences or propositions and their elements. Moreover, the notion of truth itself is so basic and all-pervasive in discourse that one should be suspicious of any attempt to define it in a completely general way. To show that a proposed definition of truth is correct or adequate would involve the use of logical reasoning which takes that concept for granted as a "primitive" or undefined notion, just as arithmetic takes the concept of number for granted.

EXERCISES

Decide whether each of the following sentences is a singular proposition and, if it is, specify what attribute its predicate assigns to the individual mentioned.

1. Happy is he who has no cares in this world.

2. The first integer larger than 100 is a prime number.

3. As a member of the Lewis and Clark expedition, Christopher Columbus discovered Japan.

4. A tall, dark and handsome man was seen walking on the beach.

5. The University of Massachusetts will conduct field-trips to the moon.

3. Attributes and Classes

There are two different ways of interpreting the notion of an attribute. One way is to think of it as a quality, property, characteristic, feature or trait; this is the "intensional" interpretation of an attribute. The other way is to think of it as a class, set, collection or group of things; this is the "extensional" interpretation. By saying that

Nixon lives in California

we may mean to say that Nixon has the characteristic of living in California, or we may mean to say that he belongs to the class of all those who live in California.

It is customary to use the word 'attribute' to refer to intensional attributes, i.e., to the intensional interpretation of attributes, and we shall follow that usage from here on. We shall use the word 'class' to refer to extensional attributes, i.e., the extensional interpretation.

The two kinds of interpretation are logically equivalent in the sense that there is no way for an individual to possess an attribute without being a member of the corresponding class, the class of all these individuals that possess that attribute. And conversely, there is no way to belong to a class without possessing some corresponding attribute, the attribute which qualifies one for membership. In this sense, the attribute of residing in California and the class of residents of California are equivalent and interchangeable notions. Anyone who has the attribute is a member of the class, and vice versa.

Does this mean that every attribute is identical with its corresponding class, or that every class is identical with its corresponding attribute? Not quite. According to traditional views, still very widely accepted, classes conform to a general principle known as the principle of <u>extensionality</u>, which may be stated most simply as follows:

No two classes have exactly the same members.

For example, the class of North-American nations and the class of English-speaking North-American Nations have exactly the same members, namely the United States and Canada. Hence, if the principle of extensionality holds, the one class must be identical with the other; they are one class rather than two. But it does not seem at all plausible to say that the (intensional) attribute of being a North-American nation is the same as the attribute of being an English-speaking North-American nation, even though the two attributes happen to apply to the same things. A North-American nation is not <u>necessarily</u> an English-speaking North-American nation. Thus if we wish to assume the principle of extensionality for classes, we have to be careful not to confuse classes with attributes.

Since we can ask whether two or more different attributes apply to the same individuals, we can also ask the converse question: can two or more individuals have exactly the same attributes? The traditional

opinion, in general, has been that they can, although
this opinion is largely rejected in modern logical
theory. The answer depends on what counts as an
"attribute". If we consider a pair of ball-bearings
turned out by a machine in perfect order, so that we
cannot distinguish them by size, shape, weight, color,
texture, and so forth, they seem to have exactly the
same attributes or properties; yet they are different.
On the other hand, one of them was turned out before
the other, or one of them was turned out in a different part of the machine, and they occupy different
places at any given moment. And these differences may
be regarded as different attributes. The theory that
some such difference can always be found is known as
the principle of the identity of indiscernibles. The
strongest form of it can be stated as follows:

No individual has every attribute possessed
by another individual.

In support of this principle, we might argue that any
given individual A has, among other attributes, the
attribute of being identical to A; hence if there is
some individual B that has every attribute belonging to
A, then B has the attribute of being identical to A, so
that A and B must be the same individual. The same
argument can be given in terms of classes rather than
attributes. Since A is a member of the class of things
identical to A, then if B is a member of every class to
which A belongs, B is a member of the class of things
identical to A.

The only plausible way to avoid this result is to
deny that there is any such attribute as the attribute
of being identical to A, or any such class as the class
of things identical to A. Attributes and classes of
this type, which apply to just one individual, are now
called unit-attributes and unit-classes. They appear
as a matter of course in modern logical systems, although their existence (as distinct from the individuals
themselves) was not generally recognized in traditional
logic or philosophy. There does not seem to be any
reason to assume that classes must have some particular
number of members or that attributes must apply to some
particular number of individuals. Modern logic, indeed
also recognizes universal attributes and classes (which
apply to everything) and empty attributes and classes
(which apply to nothing). We shall see later why this
recognition was impossible under the rules of traditional logic.

The issue of the relationship between individuals,
attributes and classes has been at stake in many fam-

ous disputes among philosophers. Some philosophers have been inclined to think that only individuals really exist and that attributes and classes are more or less convenient fictions lacking independent reality. This point of view, known as 'nominalism', was a bone of lively contention during the Middle Ages and was, in varying degrees, an important element in the British philosophical tradition since the time of Ockham. The opposing view, known as 'realism', assumes that attributes and classes have some sort of real existence, if only as mental 'concepts' or ideas. They would have to be abstract entities, that is, things having no location in space or time. Chairs and tables, for example, have space-time locations; but where or when is the attribute of being a chair, or the class of all tables? This question presents no problem if we do not assume that everything real must have a location.

The idea that two or more individuals may have exactly the same attributes suggests that there may be groups of individuals that are inter-changeable units. This idea underlies the "atomistic" philosophy developed by some of the classical Greek and Roman Philosophers (Leucippus, Democritus, Epicurus and Lucretius) and later revived by Galileo and the other founding fathers of modern physics and chemistry. According to this view, the observable characteristics of things can be explained by way of the unobserved motions and configurations of their atomic parts. Alternatively, one might deny that there are actually any fully interchangeable atomic units in nature, and one might try to account for observable characteristics by way of some theory of fields of force, or potentials, in which objects are are embedded. In many ways, the concepts of modern physical science are field-concepts (as in thermodynamics, electro-magnetic theory, relativity and quantum theory) rather than atomistic concepts. In philosophy, the same contrast can be seen in the way different philosophers have described the contents of conscious experience. According to David Hume, for instance, experience consists primarily of "impressions" and secondarily of "ideas", which are images of impressions or composites of such images; and "impressions" are interchangeable units of various types of sensation (particular colors, sounds, and so forth). Williams James, on the other hand, describes experience in terms of field-concepts.

1. What classes correspond to the following attributes?

    a. The attribute of being divisible by two.

    b. The attribute of having a step-father or
        step-mother.

    c. The attribute of being in the habit of
        committing crimes.

    d. The attribute of being an angel.

2. What attributes correspond to the following
    classes?

    a. The class of right triangles

    b. The class of persons who are fat and ugly.

    c. The class of drugs which may be purchased
        without prescription.

    d. The class of all classes of objects.

4. Negation and Obversion

For every proposition there is a corresponding
negation or denial, which is also a proposition. Thus
if

        The King rises at seven

is a propostion, then its negation,

        The King does not rise at seven,

is also a proposition. Here we have assumed, of course,
that the second sentence can function as the negation
of the first one because we take it to mean the same
thing as

        It is false that the King rises at seven.

We have to be careful, though, because sometimes the
simple transformation of an affirmative sentence into
a negative one by inserting a 'not' fails to produce
the negation of the original. For example,

            Some Senator are not Democrats

is not the negation of

            Some Senators are Democrats,

because it does not mean the same thing as

            It is false that some Senators are Democrats.

        Intuitively it seems obvious to most people that
nothing can be both true and flase (or at least not
at the same time and in the same respect). This
principle is often referred to as "the law of non-
contradiction" and as one of the fundamental "laws of
thought". Sometimes it is argued that we are quite
capable of believing contradictory pairs of propositions, although such beliefs would have to be mistaken.
And some people (mostly followers of Hegel and Marx)
go so far as to deny the validity of the principle.
But the examples offered in support of these doctrines
can always be accounted for in some orthodox and conventional way, so that they remain unconvicing except
to those predisposed to favor the doctrines. Thus it
may be argued that 'It is snowing' and 'It is not snowing' are both true, because, say, it happens to be
snowing in Oshkosh and not snowing in Beloit. The
reply would be that 'It is snowing in Oshkosh' and
'It is not snowing in Beloit' may indeed both be true,
because they are not contradictory. Most alleged
cases of contradictory truths can be handled in a
similar way. Notice also that there is no contradiction or inconsistency in believing a pair of contradictory propositions, so long as one does not believe
them at the same time.

        Another traditional "law of thought" is the
principle that every proposition is either true or
false, which is known as the "law of excluded middle".
This idea has always been more or less controversial.
If we define propositions as being whatever carries a
truth-value, and if we assume that there are just two
such values (true, false), then of course the law of
excluded middle seems trivially true. But then we
should be prepared to find that many sentences that
look like propositions may not be propositions at all,
being neither true or false. The two indicative sentences below, for instance, look very much like the
sort of sentences that might be expected to be
propositions:

The following sentence is true.

The preceding sentence is false.

Clearly, if either of the above is true, it must also be false; and if either is false, it must also be true. In this situation we must either deny that the sentences are propositions or else make room for some truth-value other than the traditional two.

Still another traditional rule, closely related to the law of excluded middle, is that if a proposition is true then its negation is false, and vice versa. This is now generally referred to as the "double nega- tion" rule. Classical logicians did not explicitly separate it from the excluded middle rule, and it has been controversial for the same reasons. It is not quite the same idea, however, for while it can be de- duced (by traditional rules) from the law of excluded middle, the latter cannot be deduced from it; and some modern logical systems possess the double negation rule without possessing the law of excluded middle.

Just as for every proposition (p) there is a corresponding proposition which is its negation ('It is false that p', or 'Not p'), so for every attribute (A) there is a corresponding attribute which is its complement ('non-A'). The complement of an attribute is the attribute of not having that attribute. Thus, to say that

This cup of tea is not sweet

is to confer the attribute of not being sweet on this cup of tea, which is the same as to say:

This cup of tea is non-sweet.

More generally, from any singular proposition of the form

x is not A

we can infer that

x is non-A

and vice versa. Note that to say that the tea is non- sweet is not the same as to say that it is bitter, which would be the "opposite" of sweet. What fails to be sweet may also fail to be bitter. Since the comple-

ment of an attribute is also an attribute, we can pass
from

    x is not non-A

to

    x is non-non-A

and vice versa. But this last form says, in effect,

    It is false that it is false that x is A,

which implies (by the double negation rule) that

    x is A.

    Naturally we can formulate these same ideas in
terms of classes rather than attributes. Thus the
complement of a class is the class of all things that
fail to belong to it. For example, from

    Nantucket is an island

we can infer

    Nantucket is not a non-island;

and vice versa, and from

    Nantucket is not an island

we can infer

    Nantucket is a non-island

and vice versa.

    These inferences, whether we make them in terms
of classes or in terms of attributes, represent the
fundamental forms of the traditional rule of obversion.
In order to state this rule clearly, we need to make a
slight change in our terminology. You will recall
that the word 'predicate', as used in speaking about
grammar, refers to one of the two basic elements in
any complete sentence, namely the verb or verb-phrase.
This part of the sentence, according to the correspondence-thesis, designates some attribute, while the
subject designates some individual (in singular propositions). But the relation of attribution is not
usually given any explicit indication, and grammatical

terminology does not provide for it. For logical
purposes, however, it is desirable to have some
standard way of representing this relation. This is
done in traditional logic by using an appropriate
form of the verb 'to be' in the present tense, which
is called the <u>copula</u> ("couple" or coupling verb) of
the proposition. What follows the copula is called
the <u>predicate term</u>, or predicate, in traditional
logic. In short: the grammatical "predicate" is
analyzed for logical purposes as being a "copula"
followed by a "predicate term". Since the copula is
always a form of the verb 'to be', the predicate
term is best thought of as the name of some class
rather than as the name of an attribute in the
intensional sense. (Otherwise, the verb 'to have'
would be more appropriate as a copula.) More pre-
cisely, in singular propositions the copula consists
of the verb 'to be', with or without the adverb 'not',
followed by the indefinite article ('a', 'an'), which
is needed before the common noun or phrase denoting
the class. Thus we have

Australia   is a   continent

(subject)   (copula) (predicate)

or, in the negative singular form,

Australia   is not a   continent.

(subject)   (copula)   (predicate)

With this understanding of the term 'predicate',
we can now formulate the traditional rule of obversion
as follows. To obtain the obverse of a proposition:

1.   Change the quality of the propostion (from
     affirmative to negative, or from negative
     to affirmative);

2.   Replace the predicate term with its comple-
     ment; if the predicate term is a complement
     ('non-P') of some other term ('P'), replace
     it with that term.

Note finally that every proposition is the same as the
obverse of its own obverse, according to these rules.
This would not be the case if the second clause of
rule 2 were omitted, or if (equivalently) the double
negation rule were rejected.

Fine the obverse of each of the following:

1. Rasputin is a monk.

2. The Grand Canal is not a highway.

3. Paris not not a non-city.

4. Greenland is a non-peninsula.

5. Distribution of terms

In traditional logic, a term in a categorical proposition was said to be <u>distributed</u> if the proposition makes some assertion (in principle) about every member of the class designated by the term; otherwise, the term was said to be <u>undistributed</u>. This distinction is important because many basic rules of traditional logic depend on it. To understand it clearly, we must remind ourselves of our theory of the structures of singular propositions.

In such propositions we always have a proper noun or definite description as subject-term, designating some individual ('N'); then we have a copula ('is a(n)', 'is not a(n)' representing the notion of class-membership; finally we have a common noun or descriptive phrase designating some class ('P'), as predicate term. In the affirmative case

N is a P,

N is asserted to be one of the members (p_1, p_2,..., p_n) of P, so that N is identical with one of those members, and one of the identity statements

$N = p_1$ (i.e., 'N is identical to p_1')

$N = p_2$

$N = p_3$

. . .

$N = p_n$

must be true. Each of these identities is an assertion about some member of P. But the affirmative singular proposition only says that one of the identities
is true, and in this sense it makes no assertion about
all members of P. Hence the predicate term of an
affirmative singular proposition may be said to be
"undistributed".

A negative singular proposition, on the other
hand,

N is not a P,

denies that N is identical with any member of P. This
means that each of the identities mentioned above must
be false; thus every member of P is different from N.
In this sense, the negative singular makes an assertion about every member of P, and its predicate term
is said to be "distributed".

Since the subject term, 'N', is the name of some
individual, the notion of distribution does not seem
to apply to it. Nevertheless, singular propositions
do appear as premises or conclusions in traditional
categorical syllogisms, and according to the rules for
such arguments it is necessary for every term to be
either distributed or undistributed. We can get
around this difficulty by adopting the convention that
the name of an individual may be treated as if it were
the name of some class having that individual as its
only member. From this point of view, the subject
term of a singular proposition (affirmative or negative) may be regarded as distributed.

We shall see later how the notion of distribution
can be extended to non-singular ("quantified") categorical propositions. This extension will result from
the fact that quantified propositions can be interpreted as abbreviations for statements about sets of
singulars, just as singulars have been interpreted as
statements about sets of identities. The idea of
interpreting quantified propositions in this way was
contained in the doctrine of "suppositions of terms",
first developed by William of Sherwood, Peter of Spain
and William of Ockham in the thirteenth century. The
doctrine of suppositions was perhaps the most important contribution to logical theory in the medieval
period. But we shall avoid the specific terminology
of this doctrine in dealing with quantified propositions.

III. MODALITY, TIME AND CHANGE

1. Basic Modal Concepts

Many philosophers, following Aristotle, distinguish two sorts of attributes that any individual possesses: "essential" ones and "accidental" ones. The essential attributes are those belonging to the individual's "essence" or species, without which it would not be the kind of thing it is; the accidental attributes come and go, so to speak, without affecting the individual's nature in any important way. This is a rather vague distinction, but it seems to have been generally accepted as part of our "common sense" view of the world. For instance, it is clear that

The number 9 is greater than the number 8

and that the attribute of being greater than the number 8 is an essential attribute of the number 9. But also

The number 9 is the number of the planets,

and here the attribute of being the number of the planets is accidental; otherwise, the fact that there are nine planets would be a fact of elementary arithmetic rather than a discovery based on astronomical observations. Or again,

The President of the U. S. A. is its chief executive

seems to assign an essential attribute to the President, while

The President of the U. S. A. is Mr. Carter

seems to assign an accidental attribute.

The distinction can be put more clearly if we say that essential attributes are those that necessarily belong to an individual; in other words (roughly) those that can be proved to belong to it. On this point of view, an essential attribute is one which is assigned by a necessarily true, or provable, proposition.

The concept of necessity as applied to propositions is a "modal" concept. It indicates a mode or
manner in which truth-value applies. We assume that
some propositions are necessarily true, for example
that

Necessarily (1 + 1 = 2),

and some are necessarily false, for example,

Necessarily not (1 + 1 = 3).

But we also assume that some propositions are neither
necessarily true nor necessarily false: they may be
true without being necessarily true, or false without
being necessarily false. Propositions of this type
are said to be contingent, i.e., contingently true or
contingently false. For example, that

Water molecules contain oxygen

is contingently true, while

Gold dissolves in water

is contingently false.

One way to understand these distinctions is to
think of them as distinctions between types of truth-
values. Instead of assuming that there are only two
truth-values ("true, "false"), we may find it more
convenient for some purposes to assume that there are
four:

Necessarily true

Contingently true

Contingently false

Necessarily false.

In modern logical theory we can handle systems based
on more than two truth-values, just as in modern geometry we can handle "spaces" with more than three di-
mensions.

The words 'necessity', 'necessary' and 'necessarily' are used in a number of different senses in every-
day life, and some of these differences will be discussed later on. What we are talking about here is the

concept of <u>logical</u> necessity. The distinguishing feature of <u>logical</u> necessity, as opposed to other concepts of necessity, is that whatever is logically necessary is also true. For this reason, logical necessity is said to be "alethic" (a-LEETH-ic). In other words, for any proposition, p, we can infer that

It is true that p

from

It is necessary that p

or

Necessarily p,

where we are using the logical or alethic sense of the words 'necessary' or 'necessarily'.

There is a close relationship between the concepts of logical necessity and logical provability, but they are not quite the same. What is logically provable depends on the axioms and rules of some "system" or theory of logic. To say that some proposition is provable is to say that it is possible to construct a "proof" (or formal argument) to establish its truth according to the rules of some logical system. A great many different systems of this kind have been proposed, and although the results in these systems agree to some extent they do not agree altogether. What is provable in one logic may not be provable in another. A system of logic is said to be <u>valid</u> if and only if every provable proposition (or "theorem") in it is necessarily true. It is said to be <u>complete</u> if and only if every necessarily true proposition is provable in it. Some systems are known to be invalid, others are known to be valid but incomplete, and others are known to be valid but not known to be complete. The question whether it is possible in principle to construct a logical system that is both valid and complete is controversial and unsettled in contemporary theory. Hence, although we can say that whatever is provable (in some valid logic) is necessary, we cannot say that whatever is necessary is provable.

The concept of <u>possibility</u> is another modal concept, closely related to the concept of necessity. What is possible, or (roughly) conceivable, may or may not be actually true; what is impossible, or incon-

ceivable, must be false. But what is false may still
be possible. Thus we can understand the notion of
possibility, like the notion of necessity, as defining
four truth-values:

    True and not possibly false

    True but possibly false

    False but possibly true

    False and not possibly true.

Intuitively, this set of values appears to be exactly
the same as the preceding one. Possibility and necessity are so intimately related, in fact, that we can
treat them as interdefinable: either one can be defined
in terms of the other. For any given proposition, p,
we can define

    Possibly p

as an abbreviation for

    Not necessarily not p;

or we can define

    Necessarily p

as an abbreviation for

    Not possibly not p.

In either case the results will be the same, and it will
turn out that any statement made in terms of necessity
can be expressed in terms of possibility, and vice versa.
Suppose that 'possibly' is the defined term. Then

    Possibly not p

in an abbreviation for

    Not necessarily not (not p),

which is equivalent by the double negation rule to

    Not necessarily p.

Working out all the basic equivalences, we obtain the
following table, where each entry in one column is

logically interchangeable with the corresponding entry
in the other column:

    Necessarily p ------------Not possibly not p

    Necessarily not p --------Not possibly p

    Not necessarily p --------Possibly not p

    Not necessarily not p ----Possibly p

    Certain relationships between the propositions in
each column are immediately obvious. The first and
third propositions on each side are incompatible,
since one of them is formulated as the negation of the
other; they cannot both be true, and if one of them is
true then the other is false. Propositions related in
this way are traditionally called contradictories.
Clearly the second and fourth propositions on each side
are also contradictories. But what is the relationship
between the first and the second, or the first and
fourth, or the second and the third, or the third and
the fourth? In order to clarify the situation, we
should first recall that we are using the alethic concept of necessity, so that we can infer 'p' from
'necessarily p' and of course 'not p' from 'necessarily
not p'. Then we should notice the corresponding property of the concept of possibility, that we can infer
'possibly p' from 'p' and similarly 'possibly not p'
from 'not p'. If 'p' were true but not 'possibly p',
then 'necessarily not p' would be true (as you can see
in the table); but this would imply that 'p' is false,
contrary to our assumption. Similarly, if 'not p' were
true but not 'possibly not p', then 'necessarily p' and
hence 'p' itself would be true.

    Now if we examine the first and fourth entries in
the left column of our table of equivalences, we see
that the first proposition logically implies the fourth.
For if

    Necessarily p

then, by the alethic rule, it follows that

    p

and hence also

    Possibly p,

which is equivalent to

    Not necessarily not p

by the table. Similarly, if the second entry is true then so is the third, i.e., if

    Necessarily not p

then

    Not p

by the alethic rule, and hence

    Possibly not p;

but this is equivalent to

    Not necessarily p.

Thus the first proposition ('Necessarily p') implies the fourth ('Not necessarily not p'), and the second ('Necessarily not p') implies the third ('Not necessarily p*'). But the converses of these implications do not hold: that is, we cannot show that the fourth implies the first or that the third implies the second. This sort of relation between propositions is called <u>subalternation</u>. The fourth proposition is the subalternate of the first, and the third proposition is the subalternate of the second. Given these results, the remaining relationships (between the first and second, and between the third and fourth) are easily established.

    A simple and elegant device for visualizing all such relationships is by the traditional "square of opposition". In the diagram below, contradictory propositions are joined by solid lines and subalternation is indicated by arrows:

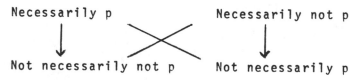

The propositions in the upper row are so related that if one of them is true then the other is false. Hence they are called <u>contraries</u>. They are not contradictories, because <u>both</u> of them may be false. Clearly if

- 36 -

necessarily p then (by subalternation) not necessarily not p, and if not necessarily not p then "Necessarily not p" is false. Similarly, if necessarily not p then 'Necessarily p' is false. The propositions in the lower row are so related that if one of them is false then the other is true. Hence they are called sub-contraries. Thus if 'Not necessarily not p' is false then its contradictory, 'Necessarily not p', is true, and therefore (by subalternation) 'Not necessarily p' is true. Both propositions, however, may be true. Finally, we can show that a proposition in the upper row is false if its subalternate is false. This is left to the reader as an exercise.

What has been shown concerning necessity-statements can also be shown for possibility-statements, given the table of equivalences. For possibility-statements we have the following square of opposition:

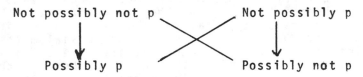

We can also combine the two kinds of modal statements in a square of opposition, for example:

EXERCISES

1. Show that if not possibly p then not necessarily p.

2. Show that if not necessarily p, and not necessarily not p, then possibly p and possibly not p.

3. Design a square of opposition for the following: 'Not necessarily not p', 'Not possibly not p', 'Not possibly p', 'Not necessarily p'.

2. Modality, Determinism and Fatalism

As the reader may have noticed, no explicit definition of 'necessity' or 'possibility' has been offered so far, although we have said that either one of these concepts could be defined in terms of the other. But one cannot provide explicit definitions for every term in logical theory any more than one can provide justifications for every type of argument or inference. Some terms must remain undefined or "primitive" so that others can be defined by means of them. On the other hand, we do have a sort of implicit definition for primitive terms, if we can specify certain rules or principles in which these terms appear and which tell us, in effect, how to use them. Our assumption that logical necessity is "alethic", for example, may serve as a rule of this kind.

Explicit definitions of the modal words have sometimes been attempted, but they have not met with complete success or approval. The interpretation of modal concepts has always been a controversial matter in philosophy, because of some puzzling difficulties that arise when we consider the relations between the modal concepts and other basic logical and philosophical concepts.

Modal concepts are important for logic because of their vital connection with the notion of valid logical proof. To say that we have a valid proof of some conclusion (C) on some set of premises (P) is to say that the truth of P guarantees the truth of C: it is not "possible" for P to be true without C also being true; if P is true, then "necessarily" C. Without these modal distinctions, we could not make sense of the notion of validity itself or explain why some things "follow logically" while others do not. Also, certain very general principles have been regarded as "laws of thought", because they have seemed inescapable and thus necessarily rather than contingently true. Among these principles, as was mentioned in the last chapter, is the "law of excluded middle", according to which every proposition is either true or false.

Some propositions indicate general characteristics or tendencies ('Dogs bark', 'There is very little snowfall in Louisiana', etc.); others indicate particular events, such as:

Jefferson wrote the Declaration of Independence.

According to the law of excluded middle, this must be true or false if it is a proposition at all. We may not know whether it is true or false. But on the assumption that it is true, there must have been some time when it was true that

Jefferson is writing the Declaration of Independence.

Before that event, presumably, it must have been true that

Jefferson will write the Declaration of Independence,

if we suppose that this sentence also is a proposition. Applied to event-descriptions in this manner, the law of excluded middle produces the fundamental form of the philosophical position known as determinism: the view that every proposition describing an event is either definitely true or definitely false at any moment of time. Hence, apparently, it was true already in the year 1770 that Jefferson was going to write the Declaration of Independence six years later. This idea seems rather strange if, as most people believe, Jefferson wrote the Declaration ultimately because he decided to do so; and in 1770 he had not perhaps even thought of it. Of course, the reply would be that he was going to think of it, as the outcome shows, although no one could have known it at the time.

But the determinist position, as we have defined it, does not quite justify this result. A proposition might be definitely true or false at all times without being definitely true at all times or definitely false at all times; its value might fluctuate back and forth, and conceivably these fluctuations might be governed by human decisions. Granting this possibility, it could be argued, the fact that a given proposition is true (or false) at a particular time is a timeless fact; hence it must be timelessly or eternally true (or false) that the proposition

Jefferson wrote the Declaration of Independence

is true at the present time. This argument seems very persuasive, although it might not stand up under careful examination. In any case, if we accept it, we obtain the position known as fatalism: the doctrine that every complete event-description is timelessly true or timelessly false.

In order to construe propositions in this timeless

way, we assume that the relation of predication (indicated by the copula) represents a timeless connection between an individual and an attribute; and if the proposition describes an event, then the specific time of the event is considered to be part of that attribute. Thus when we assign to Jefferson the attribute of writing the Declaration, we assume that this attribute is really the attribute of writing it at some particular time (1776) and that Jefferson "has" this attribute in a timeless fashion. By using the past, continuous present or future tenses, we merely specify that the time in question is earlier than, the same as or later than the time of our own utterance.

Fatalism obviously clashes with our traditional convictions about human freedom and moral responsibility. For this reason it has been a subject of passionate debate for centuries. We like to believe that the events in which we participate are determined, at least to some extent, by our own free choice between alternative courses of action; our moral evaluations of human action seem to presuppose this belief. The fatalist, of course, replies to this objection by saying that moral "freedom" is only an illusion. We think that we are fee to choose because we are unconscious of the actual motives or forces that determine our choices. According to fatalism it is silly to think that Jefferson might have chosen not to write the Declaration of Independence, just as it is silly to think that a falling stone might have chosen to disobey the law of gravitation. Unsatisfied as we may be with this position, we will probably not find any thoroughly convincing refutation of it; a determined fatalist, like a determined skeptic, can usually win the argument to his own satisfaction, if he is willing to sacrifice enough for that purpose.

From the standpoint of logic, the main problem with fatalism is that it threatens to wipe out or obscure the distinction between necessary and contingent truth. The suspicion is that whatever is timelessly true is also necessarily true. Certainly whatever we can demonstrate to be timelessly true must be necessarily true, if the demonstration is valid. Hence, for all we know, there are no timeless but contingent truths. If not, then a fatalistic philosophy which makes every truth timeless would also make every truth necessary. We need some assurance from the fatalist that his position avoids this unacceptable result.

The most plausible attempt to reconcile modal distinctions with the doctrine of fatalism is the theory of "possible worlds", which was first clearly set forth by Leibniz in the 18th century. According to this theory, the actual world is one of infinitely many possible worlds. A "possible world" is the world described by any set of propositions that is consistent, complete and coherent:

1) consistent, in that for every proposition belonging to the set, the negation of that proposition does not belong to the set; and vice versa, if the negation belongs to it, the proposition does not;

2) complete, in that for every proposition, either that proposition or its negation belongs to the set;

3) coherent, in that the logical consequences of every proposition belonging to the set also belong to the set.

Thus in every possible world Jefferson either does or does not write the Declaration of Independence, but not both; and whichever is the case in that world, so is every logical consequence of it, in conjunction with the other events in that world.

In terms of this set of conditions, we can now define our modal concepts as follows:

A necessarily true proposition is one which is true in all possible worlds.

Correspondingly, therefore,

A possibly true proposition is one which is true in at least one possible world.

Clearly a necessarily true proposition will also be actually true, since if it is true in all possible worlds, it is true in that particular possible world that happens to be the actual world. And it is easy to see how all of the relationships between modal concepts mentioned earlier in this chapter can be worked out in terms of the "possible worlds" model. At the same time, the model permits a fatalistic interpretation, since everything true in the actual world can be regarded as eternally true.

At first sight, this attempt to provide explicit definitions of modal concepts looks circular; for the notion of a "possible world" seems to presuppose the notion of possibility itself, and the notion of "logical consequence" (in the third condition) seems to presuppose the notion of validity and hence necessity itself. But in fact we do not need to make use of the modal concepts in defining the term 'possible world'. The consistency and completeness conditions, as given, do not refer to them, and we can also avoid them in spelling out the coherence condition. For we can simplify matters by assuming that we are dealing with singular propositions only, following the traditional view that all other types of propositions can be constructed from singulars; and then the "coherence" requirement will simply amount to the rule that if any proposition belongs to a possible world then so does its obverse. This will eliminate, for example, a "world" in which it would be true that Socrates is not an Athenian but false that Socrates is a non-Athenian. (Assuming, of course, that we regard the obverse as a different proposition from its original; otherwise, we can dispense with the coherence requirement altogether.)

Difficulties arise, however, when we ask which of the infinitely many possible worlds is actual and why it is actual. Leibniz himself defined the actual world as the world chosen by God, who is (he naturally assumed) all-knowing, all-powerful and all-benevolent. Then he argued that since God is benevolent He must have chosen the best; so the actual world must be "the best of all possible worlds." To the objection, How come the actual world is not perfect (since it contains murders, famines, earthquakes, etc.)?, Leibniz replied that it is as perfect as it could be; if there were a better one available, God would have actualized it. To defend himself against the obvious complaint that this position is fatalistic and thereby makes nonsense of human freedom and moral responsibility, he wrote a whole book, the Theodicy (1710). Most people have not found Leibniz' views very plausible, and they were ably lampooned in Voltaire's Candide, where Leibniz appears as the hopelessly optimistic "Dr. Pangloss".

Quite apart from the questions raised by Leibniz' speculations, however, the "possible worlds" model fails when we try to reconcile it with the traditional doctrine of singulars, the law of excluded middle, and the modal distinctions. For example, the sentence

'Jefferson wrote the Declaration of Independence'

does not qualify as a proposition at all unless there
is, in actuality, some such person as Jefferson. In
some possible worlds there is such a person; in some
there is not. Yet according to our definition of the
model, every possible world must contain the assertion
or the negation of every singular proposition. We have
tacitly assumed that there is a <u>totality</u> of all singular propositions and that each possible world selects
or rejects each member of this totality. But the notion of this totality, given the traditional doctrine
of singular propositions, makes no sense at all unless
there is also some totality of all real or actual individuals. Thus the composition of a possible world
effectively depends on some pre-established composition of the actual world, which defeats the purposes
of the model. We should have to say either

(a) that the actual individuals are the only
    possible ones, or

(b) that some possible worlds are incomplete.

In the first case, our modal distinctions collapse,
because the mere possibility of Jefferson's existence
will guarantee the truth of it. In the second case,
what collapses is the fatalistic doctrine that every
possible world, and hence the actual world, is complete.

Thus we have good reason to suspect that there
may be no satisfactory way to reconcile the doctrines
of fatalism and determinism with the modal distinctions. And modern logical theory no longer takes the
law of excluded middle, on which these doctrines depend, as a necessary logical truth.

EXERCISES

1. Assume that 'necessarily p' is defined as meaning
    'always p'. Show what meansings are thereby
    assigned to the other parts of the modal square
    of opposition ('necessarily not p', 'possible p',
    'possibly not p').

2. On the interpretation just given, whatever never
    happens is impossible. What are the disadvantages
    in this view?

3. Uses of Modal Words

The modal words that crop up frequently in every-day language do not ordinarily refer directly to the notion of logical necessity or possibility, but they can almost always be understood as indirect or elliptical ways of referring to it. We often see statements like

He has a possible skull-fracture,

which apparently invites us to contemplate a mysterious entity called a "possible skull fracture". But we avoid worrying about that by simply treating the sentence as an abbreviation for

Possibly he has a skull-fracture.

Or a statement like

Oxygen is necessarily present in combustion

means that

Necessarily oxygen is present in combustion,

although in this case we may suspect that 'necessarily' is intended to indicate something weaker than logical necessity. Statements of the type just mentioned make use of what is called modality de re, i.e., modal words applied to names of things or attributes; but these words apply more properly de dictu, to whole sentences. Modality de re is an instance of the elliptical uses of modal words, which are in practice more common than the direct or explicit logical use.

In order to understand these elliptical uses of modality, it is useful first to define the idea of consistency. Consistency can be defined in terms of the notion of possibility together with the notion of the joint truth, or conjunction, of two or more propositions. Given any two propositions, say

Henry is in charge today

and

Business is booming,

we can form the conjunction

> Henry is in charge today, and business is
> booming.

This proposition is true if and only if the given
propositions, that Henry is in charge today and that
business is booming, are both true. Since we regard
a conjunction of any two propositions as a proposition, we can apply modal words to it. So we can say,
for example,

> It is possible that Henry is in charge today
> and business is booming.

More generally, for any two propositions (p, q) we
can form the statement that

> Possibly both p and q,

and this is what is meant by saying

> p is consistent with q.

Accordingly,

> p is inconsistent with q

means

> Not possibly both p and q

or

> Necessarily not both p and q.

When we say that something is "possible", in every-
day situations, we usually do not mean that it is logically possible in and of itself but rather that is is
consistent with something else, which is not specified.
That "something else" is most apt to be some general
rule or set of rules not specified because we are taking
it for granted (for the time being) and would find it
tedious to mention it explicitly. Thus

> It is possible that Congress will pass this bill

means something like

> It is consistent with what we know about
> Congress that Congress will pass this bill.

Similar remarks apply to the every-day use of the notion

of "necessity". Oxygen is present in combustion "necessarily", not by virtue of logical necessity but becasue combustion without oxygen is inconsistent with what we know about chemistry; i.e.,

> It is inconsistent with the laws of chemistry that oxygen is not present in combustion.

In this way we obtain what may be called relative necessity and possibility in contrast to the absolute or directly logical necessity and possibility discussed earlier. Let 'L' stand for any conjunction of general rules, laws or principles in some theory or science. Then we can define 'p is necessary relative to L', or more briefly

> p is L-necessary

as meaning

> Not-p is inconsistent with L.

Hence 'p is possible relative to L', or more briefly

> p is L-possible

means

> p is consistent with L.

Relative necessity and possibility are weaker than absolute necessity and possibility because (1) we cannot infer that something is true if it is L-necessary, and (2) we cannot infer that something is L-possible if it is true. The fact that a proposition is consistent or inconsistent with 'L' does not guarantee that 'L' itself is true. If 'L' is not true, then 'p' may be false even though it is a logical consequence of 'L'. And if 'L' is not true, then 'p' may be true even though it is not consistent with 'L'. Suppose, for example, that 'L' stands for Aristotle's theory of the laws of motion, and suppose that 'p' stands for the proposition that heavier bodies fall faster than lighter ones. This proposition is a logical consequence of Aristotle's theory, in the sense that its negation (that heavier bodies do not fall faster than lighter ones) is inconsistent with the theory. But Galileo showed that the proposition is false.

Assuming that 'L' itself is consistent, and that

'p' is logically possible, we can infer that 'p' is
consistent with 'L' if its negation ('Not p') is inconsistent with 'L'. This gives us a subalternation
rule for relative necessity, analogous to the subalternation rule (above, section 1) for absolute
necessity. What is necessary relative to L must also
be possible relative to L, but not vice versa. We have
therefore a square of opposition for relative necessity
and possibility, as follows:

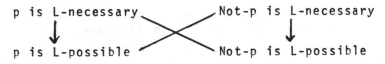

p is L-necessary   Not-p is L-necessary

p is L-possible   Not-p is L-possible

Applications of these ideas in practice are extremely numerous and varied. We have already considered some examples drawn from the natural sciences.
More generally, the notions of "cause" and "effect"
which so often appear in discussions of the sciences
may be explained by way of relative modality. These
notions will be explored later. When 'L' is allowed
to stand for some set of moral or legal rules, we
have the concepts of legal or moral necessity and
legal or moral possibility, and in these terms we can
easily define such notions as "obligation", "right',
"permission", "license", and so forth.

It is a basic provision of our legal system, for
example, that no State may deprive anyone of life,
liberty or property without due process of law (U. S.
Constitution, Amendment XIV). Hence it is "unconsti-
tutional", inconsistent with the constitution, for any
State to deprive anyone of his rights in this way. In
a similar way, we speak of certain actions as "immoral"
or "unethical", meaning that they are inconsistent with
accepted general rules of morality or ethics.

EXERCISES

1. Construct a square of opposition for the following:
   'p is permissible', Not-p is permissible', 'p is
   obligatory', 'Not-p is obligatory'. Find a specific example of these relationships.

2. Decide whether the references to "necessity" and
   "possibility" in the following statements are intended as references to absolute or to relative
   modality. If relative, to what are they relative?

1. A good Christian ought to honor his father
    and mother.

2. Odd numbers cannot be divided by 2 without
    remainder.

3. Any solid rubber ball ought to bounce.

4. If John is George's employer, then George
    must be John's employee.

5. It is impossible for anyone to memorize
    every definition in the dictionary.

4. Explanation

Modal words are frequently used in connection with
explanations. Explanation, the assignment of causes to
events, has several different forms. We explain events
in one sense, by way of regularities connecting them
with other events: in this sense, one event is said to
be a "necessary condition" or a "sufficient condition"
for another. Or we explain events teleologically in
terms of purposes, ends or goals to be realized and
the means or methods required. Or we explain them as
elements in a dynamic system, a system of objects in
space-time governed by mathematical laws. Each of
these modes of explanation has its own appropriate
sphere of application.

One event (A) is said to be a necessary condition
for another event (B), if and only if the latter (B)
cannot occur without the former (A). The word 'cannot',
in this context, indicates impossibility relative to
some set of general laws (L), not absolute impossibility. Thus if

A match burns in this bottle at t

it is a necessary condition of that event that

Oxygen is present in the bottle at t

in the sense that, for some L,

It is L-impossible that M (the match burns) and
not O (Oxygen is present).

In other words,

It is L-necessary that not both M and no O.

- 48 -

The same thing can be said more economically by using the expression

'It is L-necessary that if M then O.'

Note that we are assuming that 'M' and 'O' are propositions designating events, and we are also assuming that the latter event precedes or is simultaneous with the former. In the present case, the two events are simultaneous. But a necessary condition may be something that takes place at some earlier time. For instance, it is necessary for an egg to be fertilized before it can form an embryo. But if one event occurs later than another, it would not be regarded as a necessary condition. The formation of an embryo is not a necessary condition for fertilization. This is only a matter of convention or usage, but it reflects the fact that we think of these "conditions" as "causes"; and we tend to assume that causes, in the sense that they are represented by observable regularities, never occur later than their "effects".

A sufficient condition for an event is one that guarantees the occurrence of that event (simultaneously or at some later time). In other words, A is a sufficient condition for B if and only if, for some L,

It is L-necessary that if A then B,

where A does not occur later than B. To break an egg, it is sufficient to hit it with a sledge-hammer, although it is obviously not necessary to do so. To empty a glass of water, it is sufficient to turn it over. Some conditions are both necessary and sufficient. Thus, within certain limits, it is both necessary and sufficient to increase the length of a suspended steel spring by increasing the weight attached to it. If the weight increases, so will the length; if the weight does not increase, neither does the length.

The conception of cause-and-effect involved in these regularities is a rather weak one, although it is a basic ingredient in every-day reasoning as well as in scientific research. A regularity indicates "how" things happen in the sense that it shows them as parts of a recurring pattern or sequence. But often we are interested in knowing "why" things happen, and in that case we resort to some sort of "teleological" explanation.

Teleological explanation arises most naturally when we think about our own behavior and, by extension, human behavior in general. The fundamental ideas employed are the ideas of ends and means. To some degree I think of myself as a free agent; I can decide to do certain things "freely", without being compelled to decide one way or the other. Having decided what to do, I do it. In fact, only those things that I do "because" of having decided to do them are things that I regard as my own doing. An involuntary act, like kicking when the doctor hits my knee with his little hammer, is really no act of mine. My own acts, or sequences of acts, are deliberately done as means to achieve my chosen ends. Other events may occur between items in this sequence; some such events may have no causal relation to the main sequence, others may be side-effects of its items or accidental disruptions of its normal course. Consider for instance the following sequence of events.

1. I write a letter to a friend.

2. I hear an ambulance passing by.

3. I put the letter in a stamped envelope and address it.

4. I walk out the door and in the direction of a mail-box, carrying the letter.

5. My foot squashes a small beetle on the sidewalk.

6. A neighbor engages me in conversation for five minutes.

7. I proceed to the mail-box and drop the letter in.

The main items in this sequence (1, 3, 4, 7) are results of my decision to send a message, by letter, to my friend. Each of these items is a means to that end. Since presumably I have some reason for wanting to send the message, that "end" is a means to some further end (such as getting him to do me some favor). The initial item, my writing the letter, is possible only because I have letter-writing materials at hand; their presence is a "means" to writing the letter. Thus the sequence as a whole is embedded in some larger sequence. Within this larger sequence, it serves as an "end" relative to what precedes it and as a "means" relative to what follows it. More generally, we can regard each main item of any purposive sequence as being both an end and a means in this sense. Other items, like numbers 2, 5 and 6 in the example, play no essential part in this particular sequence but may play some such part in a different one, i.e., in connection with activities of some other person or stages in some natural process.

It will be noticed that the order of events in the main sequence is crucial: I cannot put the letter in the envelope, and so on, until after I have written the letter. Writing it is a necessary condition for mailing it. To this extent, the idea of a teleological sequence seems to coincide with the idea of regularity previously discussed. Certainly, if I could not count on regular connections between certain pairs of events, I could not sensibly choose a course of action as a "means" to achieve my purposes. To qualify as a means, an event must be either a necessary condition or a sufficient condition for my chosen end. But this does not guarantee that it will actually take place, even though I have decided that it will. I may decide to write a letter, find myself distracted by some intervening problem or accident, and never get around to writing the letter. My choosing to write the letter is, as lawyers say, a sine qua non; but still I must deliberately carry out each step in the process.

Thus a teleological sort of explanation differs from an explanation in terms of regularities in three fundamental ways : (1) the event to be explained must have been chosen and brought about by some person (or other agent) capable of choosing and acting; (2) it must be an item in some sequence of acts governed by purposes or ends; (3) these ends are events occurring in the future, relative to the event in question, not the past. We do things in order to bring something about in the future; that is why we do them.

Classical philosophers laid great emphasis on this type of explanation and extended it to cover all sorts of phenomena. If I think of my own behavior in teleological terms, it is very natural and easy to extend that way of thinking by analogy to all human beings; I attribute to them thoughts, feelings and motives similar to my own. I can go a step further by assuming that it is possible to choose ends and means without doing so consciously, and in this way I can extend teleological explanation to the behavior

of animals, plants and organisms generally. Even the
parts or organs of living bodies can be viewed as if
they were designed to perform some particular function,
i.e., as means to certain ends (respiration, digestion,
reproduction, etc.). Having gone this far, I might
also want to apply the ends-means analysis to inorganic
nature: the behavior of chemical substances, the motions of the stars and planets. Thus Aristotle ascribes
a "natural motion" to each of the chemical "elements",
(earth, water, air, fire), whereby each element strives
to attain its end, to return to its "natural" place in
the universe if it has been displaced. In order to
account for the apparently circular motions of the
heavenly bodies, he postulated a fifth "element",
aether, whose constant circular motion was supposedly
an effort to emulate the static perfection of God
(the Unmoved Mover).

Used as a general principle for all types of
events, the traditional teleological theory amounts
to a cosmic anthropomorphism: it pictures the world as
a whole in terms of human or quasi-human actions and
motivations. This way of thinking has its good and
bad points. Its attraction is its simplicity and uni-
formity, apart from the fact that it flatters our self-
image. One can apply it in every branch of philosophy,
from physics and astronomy to psychology, ethics,
politics and art-criticism. Its most obvious weakness
is that we really have no good reason to suppose that
every event or process in nature is governed by something similar to human choices and purposes. In order
to sustain this view, one has to postulate all sorts
of hidden ("occult") powers and instincts in things.
It is not possible to devise experiments or make observations that will definitely show the presence or
absence of such occult powers; for this would depend
on being able to predict, in principle, that given
such-and-such a motivation there would follow such-and-
such a behavioral effect at some definite time. But
we have seen that even in connection with human behavior, where they are most plausible, teleological
explanations do not give us reliable grounds for
definite predictions. After we have done something,
we can show with some plausibility why we did it; but
before it happens, various accidents may occur to
prevent it. Thus teleological explanation is relatively useless for the purposes of experimental science,
and it is no accident that it has been abandoned in
those areas of the philosophy of nature -- physics,
chemistry and, more recently, biology -- where the
methods and ideas of experimental science are strongly
established.

The kind of explanation favored in the experimental sciences (at least as an ideal, if not actually attained) is explanation in terms of dynamic systems. A dynamic system is a set of objects or entities located in space and time, or space-time, whose behavior is governed completely by some set of mathematically formulated laws. At any given moment of time, the objects of the system are supposed to have some definite location, and other definite characteristics (such as mass, velocity, electrical charge, energy), which define the "state of the system" at that time. Once any state of the system is completely defined, the laws of the system specify exactly what every other state of the system is. This is what makes the system "dynamic". A static system (or "statics"), on the other hand, is one which furnishes a complete specification of a state on the basis of a partial description.

One of the simplest examples of a dynamic system is the set of relatively large bodies known as the solar system. The objects of this system are the sun, the earth, eight other planets, various moons or satellites, and asteroids. Assuming (by a convenient fiction) that the sun occupies a fixed position in space, we define the motions of the other objects in terms of orbits around the sun, or orbits around the larger planets. Each of these bodies is assumed to have a definite position, mass and velocity at all times, and the numbers representing these quantities define the state of the system at any time. The laws of planetary motion, derived from Newton's law of universal gravitation and general laws of motion, determine any state of the system from a given state. (This is true, however, only with certain qualifications. The classical theory of the solar system did not account for the rotation of the orbit of the planet Mercury, for example, a defect which was corrected by Einstein's general theory of relativity.)

Thus the theory of the solar system as a dynamic system "explains" the observed behavior of the planets and other bodies in their neighborhood in the sense that it reduces this behavior to mathematical rules which permit extensive and precise predictions. Of course, this theory tells us nothing about the relations of the solar system as a whole to the larger astronomical systems (the local galaxy, systems of galaxies) in which it participates; and it disregards the possible effects of objects or events in the neighborhood which are not defined as parts of the system (such as events on or within the earth which might affect its motion). A space-vehicle taking off from the earth's surface presumably has some effect on the rotation and orbit of the earth itself, although for most purposes one would treat such effects as negligible.

The concept of dynamic systems operates as an ideal for the natural sciences. It provides the kind of orderly picture of events that one would like to achieve; but it is not often actually achieved. In the theory of gases, for example, one would like to be able to think of gas particles as if they formed some sort of orderly quasi-planetary system, but there are too many of them and too many unknown factors and complications. Hence the theory of gases is actually formulated in terms of probability theory, which permits one to deal effectively with the behavior of large numbers of objects without having to take account of what each individual object is doing. The same principle is used by insurance companies in evaluating risks.

Some scientists and philosophers have believed that the universe as a whole, in principle, is a dynamic system, even though we do not (and presumably never will) fully understand its laws. The most famous and striking statement of this view was given by the great French mathematician and astronomer the Marquis Pierre Simon de Laplace (1749-1827), in a book on the mathematical theory of probability. He suggested that a sufficiently powerful intelligence, knowing the positions of all material bodies in the universe at some given instant, and knowing all the forces acting at that instant, would be able to determine exactly what had happened or what would happen at any other instant, past or future.

This vision of the universe as a sort of gigantic clockwork-mechanism is, of course, radically opposed to the older teleological point of view discussed earlier. It did seem to be implicit in the Newtonian mathematical physics of Laplace's era. Since then, however, scientific theory has developed in ways not particularly congenial to this mechanistic vision. According to relativity theory, there is no such thing as a simultaneous "state of the system" for the whole universe at any instant; and according to quantum physics, there is a fundamental indeterminacy in the positions or momenta (or both) of the elementary particles of matter at any time.

None of the three general types of explanation we have considered seems to be adequate for all situations or purposes. But we have no good reason to suppose that it would be. What may be true or significant for certain kinds of phenomena may not be true or significant for others. By what right could we assert that the laws governing human behavior, or animal behavior, must be comparable to the laws of motion for planets, galaxies, molecules or electrons? Lawfulness itself, on the other hand, is in some sense a common ingredient in all forms of explanation. An event which exhibits no lawful connections to other events has no "explanation" at all. We might give it a quasi-explanation by calling it an "act of God".

But what are the "laws" that provide us with the "lawfulness" required by our various modes of explanation? And how do we come to know them or believe in them? They are obviously of different sorts; some have a mathematical form, for example, and others do not. One characteristic they all have in common; they are universal propositions. They do not deal with particular individuals but rather with all individuals, or with all members of some class of individuals. In order to understand them, we must now extend the apparatus of our logic.

IV. QUANTIFICATION AND IMMEDIATE INFERENCE

1. Quantified Propositions

As noted earlier (chapter II), some propositions are categorical, being simple sentences; and we divided the class of categorical propositions into two sub-classes, namely, singular propositions and quantified propositions. A quantified proporition assigns an attribute, not to some single specified individual but to all, or some, unspecified members of a class. Like a singular, a quantified proposition may be either affirmative or negative; it may also be either univer-sal or particular. Hence we have four traditionally recognized types of quantified propositions: universal affirmative, like

All horses are quadrupeds;

universal negative, like

No marsupials are reptiles;

particular affirmative, like

Some Congressmen are Republicans,

and particular negative, like

Some poets are not professors.

The traditional rules for handling quantified pro-positions were based on the idea that we can interpret them as abbreviations for statements about sets of sin-gulars. This idea can be spelled out as follows. Let 'S' represent the subject-term and 'P' the predicate-term in any quantified proposition, and let the members of their corresponding classes be represented in the usual way ('s_1', 's_2', 'p_1', 'p_2', etc.). Then we can write down a set of singular propositions corresponding to the members of S:

s_1 is a P
s_2 is a P
s_3 is a P
. . . . .
s_n is a P

Each of the four types of quantified propositions can be interpreted in terms of this set. The universal affirmative, of the general form

All S are P,

will be understood to assert that _every_ member of the set is true. The universal negative,

No S are p,

asserts that _no_ member of the set is true; i.e., every member is false. The particular affirmative,

Some S are P,

asserts that _at least one_ member of the set is true. The particular negative,

Some S are not P,

asserts that _at least one_ member of the set is _not_ true, i.e., false.

We are assuming that each member of the set is a genuine singular proposition and that it satisfies the law of excluded middle (must be either true or false). Consequently, we have an alternative but equivalent method of interpreting the negative quantified propositions, using a set of negative singulars:

s_1 is not a P

s_2 is not a P

s_3 is not a P

. . . . .

s_n is not a P.

We can take the universal negative as asserting that every member of this negative set is true; and we can take the particular negative as asserting that at least one member of the negative set is true. In practice, it will be simpler to interpret the negative quantified propositions in this way.

In order to be able to talk about these propositions without having to use cumbrous locutions, we
shall adopt the following traditional abbreviations:

A universal affirmative proposition will be
called an 'A-proposition'.

A universal negative proposition will be
called an 'E-proposition'.

A particular affirmative proposition will be
called an 'I-proposition'.

A particular negative proposition will be
called an 'O-proposition'.

The use of these letters (A, E, I, O) was suggested by
the vowels in the Latin words 'affirmo' ("I affirm")
and 'nego' ("I deny").

Now consider the relationships between these four
propositional types.

It is obvious that if an A-proposition is true
then the corresponding I-proposition must also be true.
For the A-proposition asserts that every member of the
set of affirmative singulars is true, and the I-proposition asserts that at least one of those singulars
is true. The converse does not hold, since one or
more of the singulars may be true even though not all
of them are true. Thus the relationship between A and
I is <u>subalternation</u>: the I-proposition is the subalternate of the A-proposition. For instance, if it
is true that

All judges are lawyers

then it follows by subalternation that

Some judges are lawyers;

but not vice versa. Note that if we say "Some judges
are lawyers" in ordinary conversation we are usually
understood as implying that some judges are <u>not</u> lawyers;
but in traditional logical terminology, the word 'some'
does not carry this implication.

Similar reasoning shows that the E-proposition and
the O-proposition are also related by subalternation:
the O is the subalternate of the E.

Thus if

      No Republicans are Democrats

it follows that

      Some Republicans are not Democrats,

but not vice versa.

    The A-proposition and the corresponding O-proposition are <u>contradictories</u>, since they must have opposite truth-values. If every member of the set of affirmative singulars is true, as the A-proposition asserts, then it is false that one or more of them is not true; and if it is false that one or more of them is not true, then all of them are true. Moreover, if it is false that all of them are true, then at least one of them is not true; and vice versa. For example, the proposition that

      All Senators are citizens

is contradictory to the proposition that

      Some Senators are not citizens.

    By similar reasoning, the E-proposition and the I-proposition are contradictories. For example, the proposition that

      No democracies are dictatorships

is contradictory to the proposition that

      Some democracies are dictatorships.

    Given these relationships, it is clear that we can form a square of opposition for the four types of quantified propositions as follows:

Or, more simply:

Since we have a square of opposition for these propositions, we can easily show that the two universals (A,
E) are contraries: if one of them is true, the other
is false (cf. chapter III). This is because if the A
is true then (by subalternation) so is the I; but if
the I is true then (by contradiction) the E is false;
hence, if A then not E. We might represent this proof
schematically as follows:

1. A   hypothesis

2. I   1, subalternation

3. Not E   2, contradiction

The line drawn under step 1 serves to remind us that
this proposition is not necessarily true but is merely
assumed for the sake of argument. Naturally, a similar short proof would show that if the E-proposition
is true then the A-proposition is false. On the hypothesis 'E', we can derive 'Not A'. The two proofs
taken together then establish that the universals are
contraries. They are not contradictories, of course,
because they may both be false; that is, we cannot
show that 'E' follows from 'Not A', or that 'A'
follows from 'Not E'.

By similar reasoning, we can show that the two
particular propositions (I, O) are sub-contraries:
if one of them is false, the other is true; but they
may both be true. Thus if the I is false, its contradictory (E) is true; and then (by subalternation)
the O is also true. Similarly, if not O, then I.

Finally, we can show that if the I is false the
A is false; and if the O is false the E is false.
This is a sort of inversion of the subalternation
relation, which might be called superalternation
(some texts call it 'superimplication'). Proof is
left to the reader.

The traditional square of opposition does not
really represent the way we use quantified propositions in every-day talk. As was mentioned earlier,
when I say that some S are P I usually mean to imply
that some S are not P, and vice versa. Thus I normally use the particular affirmative and particular
negative forms as if they were equivalent to each
other. In that case, the traditional rules for the
square of opposition break down almost completely,
and what I actually have is a sort of triangle of

opposition, as follows:

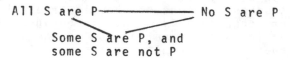

All S are P ——————————— No S are P

Some S are P, and
some S are not P

where each proposition is contrary (but not contradictory, sub-contrary, subalternate or superalter-
nate) to each of the others.

Since this scheme is much simpler than the
traditional square, why was it not adopted in logical
theory? Probably the answer is that there are, after
all, occasions when we want to say that some S are P
without committing ourselves to the idea that some of
them are not, and vice versa. We know that some of
the planets in our solar system contain life, because Earth does; but surely this does not guarantee
that some of the other planets do not contain life.
The square of opposition is more adequate than the
triangle, because it takes into account both the
possibility that the I and O propositions have the
same value, which the triangle takes for granted, and
the possibility that they do not.

EXERCISES

1. Make a complete list of all the valid inferences
   that can be made in the square of opposition,
   using the 'If...then - - -' form (e.g., 'If A
   then not E').

2. Prove that the two affirmative propositions (A, I)
   and the two negative propositions (E, O) are related by superalternation.

3. What can be validly inferred in the square of opposition from each of the following?

   a. All precious stones are gems.

   b. It is false that some parrots are mathema-
       ticians.

   c. Some crustaceans are not lobsters.

   d. It is false that no Armenians are bishops.

2. Obversion and Conversion

Since every singular proposition has an obverse which is logically equivalent to it (see chapter II), it is clear that every set of singulars of the form

s_1 is a P, etc.

must be equivalent to some corresponding set of the obverses of those singulars, i.e.,

s_1 is not a non-P

s_2 is not a non-P

s_3 is not a non-P

. . . .

s_n is not a non-P.

If the first set is a set of true propositions, as expressed by the universal affirmative

All S are P,

then the second set must also consist of true propositions, expressed by the universal negative

No S are non-P,

which is the <u>obverse</u> of the universal affirmative. Also, the propositions in the first set are obverses of those in the second set, so that the universal affirmative is the obverse of the universal negative. They are obverses of each other.

For the same reason, we regard

Some S are P

and

Some S are not non-P

as obverses of each other. Likewise,

No S are P

and

> All S are non-P

are obverses; and so are

> Some S are not P

and

> Some S are non-P.

The general rule for constructing obverses of quantified propositions is the same as the rule for constructing obverses of singulars: namely,

1. Change the quality of the proposition;

2. Replace the predicate term with its complement.

Using specific examples of subject and predicate terms, we can show all of the basic cases of pairs of obverses in a table, as follows:

All citizens are voters	No citizens are non-voters
No citizens are voters	All citizens are non-voters
Some citizens are voters	Some citizens are not non-voters
Some citizens are not voters	Some citizens are non-voters

Each proposition is the obverse of the corresponding proposition in the other column and is logically equivalent to it. Clearly we can construct a square of opposition for the propositions in the right-hand column as well as for the others. But we can also validly infer the truth (or untruth) of any entry from the truth (or untruth) of its obverse in the other column. This provides us with a kind of inference not found in the square of opposition.

Quantified propositions have another important characteristic, however, which is not present in singular propositions. A quantified proposition has a converse, which is obtained by simply reversing the

order of its subject and predicate terms. The results
can be seen in the following table, where each entry
is the converse of the corresponding entry in the
other column:

All S are P	All P are S
No S are P	No P are S
Some S are P	Some P are S
Some S are not P	Some P are not S.

But converses are not in general logically equivalent;
in some cases they are, and in some they are not. E-
propositions and I-propositions are equivalent to their
converses, but A-propositions and O-propositions are
not. The reasons for this situation can be seen by
examining the appropriate sets of singulars.

Just as, for the E-proposition 'No S are P', we
have a set of negative singulars of the form

s_1 is not a P, etc.,

so for its converse, 'No P are S', we have

p_1 is not an S, etc.

Clearly the two E-propositions must be equivalent if
the corresponding sets of singulars are equivalent.
Now the reader may recall (from chapter II) that we
can interpret a singular proposition as an abbreviated
way of saying that all (or some) of a set of identity-
statements are true (or false). Thus we interpret
's_n is not a P' as a way of saying that each of the
statements

$$s_n = p_1$$

$$s_n = p_2$$

$$s_n = p_3$$

. . . .

$$s_n = p_m$$

(where S has n members and P has m members) is false.
But identity is a symmetrical relation, so that in
general 'a = b' is logically equivalent to 'b = a' and

either one of these identities can be validly inferred from the other.   Hence we also have the equivalent set

$$p_1 = s_n$$

$$p_2 = s_n$$

$$p_3 = s_n$$

. . . .

$$p_m = s_n$$

which must have the same truth-value as the other.   For
each member of S we have a set of each type, and accord
ing to the original E-proposition each of the identity-
statements in all of these sets must be false.   So
there are n sets of the second type as well as n sets
of the first type; if we wanted to write down those of
the second type, we would get an array like the following:

$$p_1 = s_1 \quad p_1 = s_2 \quad p_1 = s_3 \quad \cdots \quad p_1 = s_n$$

$$p_2 = s_1 \quad p_2 = s_2 \quad p_2 = s_3 \quad \cdots \quad p_2 = s_n$$

$$p_3 = s_1 \quad p_3 = s_2 \quad p_3 = s_3 \quad \cdots \quad p_3 = s_n$$

$$\cdots \qquad \cdots \qquad \cdots \qquad \cdots \qquad \cdots$$

$$p_m = s_1 \quad p_m = s_2 \quad p_m = s_3 \quad \cdots \quad p_m = s_n$$

Since each of these identities is false, we know that
each of the identities in each of the horizontal rows
is false; and each horizontal row can be written down
in our normal vertical fashion, e.g.,

$$p_1 = s_1$$

$$p_1 = s_2$$

$$p_1 = s_3$$

. . .

$$p_1 = s_n.$$

Since each of these identities is false, the singular
proposition 'p_1 is not an S' must be true.   Likewise,
all of the other singulars in the set represented by

the E-proposition 'No P are S' must be true. Hence
that proposition must be true if its converse 'No S
are P' is true.

By similar reasoning we can easily show that an
I-proposition is equivalent to its converse. The I-
proposition asserts that at least one of the set

s_1 is a P, etc.

is true. Hence at least one of the entries in the
array of identity-statements must be true, which means
that at least one of the horizontal rows contains one
or more true statements. Therefore, at least one of
the singulars

p_1 is an S, etc.

must be true, so that 'Some P are S' is logically
equivalent to 'Some S are P'.

These results are intuitively obvious in concrete examples. It seems obvious that if it is true
that

No stars are planets

then it is also true that

No planets are stars;

and likewise, if

Some politicians are conservatives

then

Some conservatives are politicians.

But it seems equally clear that if

All women are people

it does not follow that

All people are women;

and if

Some people are not women

it does not follow that

Some women are not people.

The reason why an A-proposition is not equivalent to its converse is that it asserts only that every member of its subject-class (S) is identical with some member of its predicate-class (P), and it does not follow from this that every member of P is identical with some member of S. P might have more members than S. In the case of an O-proposition, the assertion is that some member of S is not identical with any member of P; but this could be true even though every member of P were identical with some member of S, since S might have more members than P. Hence the converse O-proposition, that some member of P are not members of S, does not follow.

The traditional way of accounting for these facts about the converses of quantified propositions is in terms of the notion of distribution. We saw (chapter II) that the predicate term in a negative singular proposition is said to be "distributed" because, in effect, the proposition makes an assertion about every member of the predicate class. By the same token, the predicate term in any negative quantified proposition, universal or particular, is distributed. Such a proposition asserts that at least one or all of some set of negative singulars is true, and each of those singulars has a distributed predicate term. But in addition, the subject term in any universal proposition is distributed. A universal asserts that every member of some set of singulars, affirmative or negative, is true, and this is an assertion about every member of the subject class.

Thus each of the four quantified propositions has its own pattern of distribution. In the A-proposition the subject, but not the predicate, is distributed; in the E-proposition both terms are distributed; in the O-proposition the predicate, but not the subject; and in the I-proposition neither term. These different patterns give us a convenient shorthand method for representing the different propositional forms. Let us call it "distribution shorthand". We shall use capital letters ('S', 'P') to represent distributed terms and lower-case letters ('s', 'p') to represent undistributed terms. Then each type of quantified proposition can be expressed simply by juxtaposing two appropriate letters in such

a way that the first letter represents the subject
term and the second represents the predicate term,
as in the following table.

A-proposition (All S are P) : Sp

E-proposition (No S are P) : SP

I-proposition (Some S are P) : sp

O-proposition (Some S are not P) : sP

Now we can restate the table of converses (see
above) in terms of this shorthand, so that the patterns
of distribution stand out clearly:

Sp   Ps

SP   PS

sp   ps

sP   pS

Notice that in the middle rows (E and I-propositions)
the distribution of subject and predicate terms does
not change as one moves from a given form to its converse. In these cases, the converses are logically
equivalent. In the first and fourth rows, however,
the status of each term changes. The predicate of
the A-proposition, undistributed in the original, is
"promoted" to the status of being distributed in the
converse; and the subject of the O-proposition is
likewise promoted in the converse. These promotions
are illicit, in the sense that they presume more information than the original proposition conveys.
Hence the converse propositions of these forms are
not equivalent and cannot be validly inferred from
each other.

The distribution shorthand can now be extended
in a very simple way so as to represent the operations
of obversion. We shall use a horizontal bar over a
letter ('$\bar{S}$', '$\bar{s}$', etc.) to form the complement of the
term represented by that letter. Now we can restate
the table of obversions as follows:

Sp	S$\overline{\text{P}}$
SP	S$\overline{\text{p}}$
sp	s$\overline{\text{P}}$
sP	s$\overline{\text{p}}$

In terms of the shorthand, the operations involved in obversion take the following form:

1. Place (or remove) a bar over the predicate letter;

2. Change the size of the predicate letter.

You will have noticed that changes in quality (affirmative, negative) are expressed in the shorthand by changes in size of the predicate letter.

EXERCISES

For each of the following propositions, write down (a) its obverse, (b) its converse, (c) its representation in traditional form ('All S are P', etc., using the subject and predicate letters suggested in each case), (d) the traditional representations of its obverse and converse, and (e) the representations of each in distribution shorthand ('Sp', 'S$\overline{\text{p}}$', etc., again using the suggested letters).

1. No scholars are politicians. (S, P)

2. Some books are novels. (B, N)

3. All fractions are ratios. (F, R)

4. Some doctors are not magicians. (D, M)

3. Derived Forms of Inference

The rules for the square of opposition, obversion and conversion provide us with a set of basic valid forms of immediate inference. These inferences are said to be "immediate" because in making them we pass directly from some individual proposition, taken as a premise and without the help of any other premises, to a conclusion. The forms examined so far are "basic" in the sense that they are assumed as primitive

or underived argument-forms in most presentations of
traditional logic. In fact, we have derived them from
our interpretation of quantified propositions in terms
of singulars. From these basic forms of inference,
several others can now be derived.

The derived forms result from combining the
operations of obversion, conversion and the square of
opposition in various ways.

First, although the A-proposition is not equivalent to its converse, its subalternate (an I-proposition) does have an equivalent converse. Therefore,
since we can infer the subalternate from the universal,
we can infer the converse of the subalternate as well.
Thus we have

    1. All S are P   hypothesis

    2. Some S are P   1, subalternation

    3. Some P are S   2, conversion

The last proposition is the converse by limitation of
the first. For example, given that

    All Swedes are Scandinavians

we can infer its converse by limitation,

    Some Scandinavians are Swedes,

even though we cannot infer its real converse ('All
Scandinavians are Swedes'). This amounts to a derived
form of inference:

    1. All S are P   hypothesis

    2. Some P are S   1, conversion by limitation

In the shorthand form

    1. Sp

    2. ps

or more simply

    Sp
    ps

we see clearly that no illicit promotion of terms has
occurred.

An important group of derived inferences results from performing obversions and conversions
alternatively from any given quantified proposition.
Suppose we have

1. <u>All spruces are conifers</u>   hypothesis

2. No spruces are non-conifers 1, obversion

We could obvert the second proposition now, but this
would merely reproduce the hypothesis itself. If we
convert it, however, we get a new proposition:

3. No non-conifers are spruces   2, conversion

Conversion of this proposition would give us number
2 again, but by obversion we obtain

4. All non-conifers are non-spruces

which is known as the <u>contrapositive</u> of the original
hypothesis (step 1). In general, every quantified
proposition has a contrapositive, if we define
'contrapositive' as the result of an operation of
"contraposition", namely the operation of replacing
both terms of the converse of a given proposition by
their complements. These results appear in the
following table:

All S are P	All non-P are non-S
No S are P	No non-P are non-S
Some S are P	Some non-P are non-S
Some S are not P	Some non-P are not non-S

Each entry is the contrapositive of the corresponding
entry in the other column. But the contrapositives
are equivalent to each other only in the first and
fourth lines, not in the middle lines. Thus for the
O-opposition we have

1. <u>Some S are not P</u>   hypothesis

2. Some S are non-P   1, obversion

3. Some non-P are S   2, conversion

4. Some non-P are not non-S 3, obversion

But we do not have similar proofs for the E and I-propositions. For the I-proposition we have

1. Some S are P   hypothesis

2. Some S are not non-P 1, obversion

Since step 2 is an O-proposition, its converse does not follow and the chain of inferences by alternating obversion and conversion stops short. For the E-proposition we have

1. No S are P   hypothesis

2. All S are non-P   1, obversion

and again we cannot proceed to the converse of step 2. However, we do have

3. Some non-P are S   2, conversion by
                                limitation

4. Some non-P are not non-S 3, obversion

where step 4 is the contrapositive of the subalternate ('Some S are not P') of the hypothesis. It is know as the <u>contrapositive by limitation</u> of the E-proposition.

In distribution shorthand, the table of contrapositives is

Sp $\overline{Ps}$

SP $\overline{PS}$

sp $\overline{ps}$

sP $\overline{pS}$

which differs from the table of converses only in that there is a bar over each letter in the right-hand column. The reader may have noticed that the properties of contrapositives are a sort of mirror-image of the properties of converses. Just as E and I have equivalent converses, so A and O have equivalent contrapositives; and as A has a converse by limitation which can be validly inferred from it, so E has a contrapositive by limitation which can be validly inferred.

As we extended the chain of inferences from the E-proposition by the use of conversion by limitation, so we can also extend the chain of the A-proposition. Thus from

1. **All S are P**   hypothesis

2. All non-P are non-S   1, contraposition

we can proceed to

3. Some non-S are non-P   2, conversion by limitation

4. Some non-S are not P   3, obversion

which is known as the <u>inverse</u> of the hypothesis. Every quantified proposition has an inverse if we define the operation of "inversion" as being the operation of replacing the subject term of the contradictory of a proposition by its complement. The reader should now be able to formulate the inverses of the remaining types of propositions (E, I, O) and decide which of them, if any, can be validly inferred from these propositions.

EXERCISES

Write down representations in traditional form and in distribution shorthand for each of the propositions below, and show which of them may be inferred from the first one on the list.

1. All writers are readers. (W, R)

2. No writers are non-readers.

3. All readers are writers.

4. Some readers are writers.

5. All non-readers are non-writers.

6. No readers are non-writers

7. Some non-writers are not readers.

8. All non-writers are non-readers.

9. Some non-readers are not non-writers.

10. Some readers are not non-writers.

4. Induction

In order to know that a particular (I, O) proposition is true, it suffices to know that one of its corresponding set of singulars is true. If I know that one individual book is a biography, then I have all the information needed to draw the inference that some books are biographies. But universal (A, E) propositions raise a more difficult problem. The universal asserts that every one of its corresponding set of singulars is true, and in many cases this set is so large that I have no way of obtaining all the necessary information about its members. Of course, I may be able to infer the universal from some other universal already established or taken for granted, using the patterns of reasoning discussed above or others like them.

Sometimes, however, even though I have not examined every member of a large set of singulars I may be able to show that all of them are true. The basic method for doing this has been familiar to mathematicians for a long time. It is called mathematical induction. This method of reasoning is very powerful, but it works only under three rather stringent conditions:

1. The individuals designated by the subject terms of the singulars must form a well ordered series.

2. If any of these individuals has the property (or belongs to the class) designated by the predicate term, then so does its immediate successor in the series.

3. The first individual in the series has this property.

If a set of singular propositions meets all of these conditions, all of its members must be true, and so is the universal proposition corresponding to it. To see why, we must examine the notion of a "well ordered series".

The simplest example of a well-ordered series is the series of positive whole numbers, or positive integers (1, 2, 3, ..., n, n+1,...). The integers are said to form a series because they are all related to each other in such a way that the relation between them is asymmetrical, transitive and connected. This relation is expressed by the phrase, '...is larger than...'. It is an asymmetrical relation because, for any pair of integers (x, y),

> if x is larger than y, then y is <u>not</u> larger than x.

It is a transitive relation because, for any three integers (x, y, z),

> if x is larger than y, and y is larger than z, then x is larger than z.

It is a connected relation because, for any two integers (x, y),

> either x is larger than y, or y is larger than x.

These properties can easily be verified by substituting any randomly chosen integers for 'x', 'y' and 'z' (provided of course that they are different integers). The series is said to be well-ordered, because any group (or sub-set) of terms chosen from it always has a "first" term: that is, a term that is not larger than any other term in the sub-set. For example, the "first" term in the sub-set

256,9,103

is 9. and it is easy to see that every randomly chosen set of integers will have a first, or smallest, term in this way.

Since the class of positive integers forms a well-ordered series, any class of things that can be put into a one-to-one correspondence with the integers, or with some sub-set of the integers, is also a well-ordered series. A "one-to-one correspondence" of things to integers is simply any way of assigning integers to things so that each thing has one and only one integer assigned to it. You will notice that our "extensional" treatment of attributes as classes of individuals (cf. chapter II) presumes that we can regard these individuals as forming some sort of well-ordered series. It amounts to the assumption that each individual member of a class has, in principle, some particular name or number not assigned to any other member.

Although it is obviously impossible to prove

general laws about all positive integers by inspecting each number individually, we can show a great deal about them by mathematical induction. For example, we can show that for every integer there is at least one corresponding term in the series of positive even integers (2, 4, 6,..., m, m+2,...), such that the latter term is twice as large as the former. In order to do this we show

(I)   that if any even integer (m) is twice as large as some given integer (n), so that m = 2n, then there is some other even integer which is twice as large as the immediate successor (n + 1) of n.

This is not difficult to show, since we know that the successor of m in the series of even integers (m + 2) is twice as large as n + 1:

$$m + 2 = 2n + 2 = 2(n + 1).$$

Next we show

(II)   that there is some even integer which is twice as large as the first integer (1).

This is obviously true, since the first even integer (2) is twice as large as the first integer. But now it follows that <u>every</u> positive integer has this property, i.e., the property assigned to the first integer in part II of the demonstration above. This is because we know from part I that

if some even integer is twice as large as the first integer, then some other even integer is twice as large as its immediate successor (the second integer).

But we know from part II that

some even integer is twice as large as the first integer;

hence

some even integer is twice as large as the second integer.

Then by similar reasoning we can show that

some even integer is twice as large as the third integer; and so on, in principle, <u>ad infinitum</u>.

It would be nice if we could establish all sorts of universal propositions by the method of mathematical induction, or something like it. But when we try to apply it outside the orderly domain of pure mathematics or logical theory we find that one or more of its prerequisite conditions cannot be satisfied. First, we may not always be able to show, or safely assume, that our classes of individuals are well ordered. But even if we could always make this assumption, we have no way of knowing in general that if the nth individual in a series has some property then the $n + 1^{th}$ individual also has it. For example, assuming that we can regard the class of all swans as forming a well ordered series (perhaps by reference to their dates and places of birth), we might be able to discover that

Swan$_1$ is white

Swan$_2$ is white

. . . .

Swan$_n$ is white

up to some particular finite number (n) of swans; but we have no way of knowing that if any individual swan is white then its successor in the series is also white. Thus the universal generalization that

All swans are white

would be hazardous at best; and in fact we know now that some swans are not white, since black swans have been discovered.

Most of the generalizations we make in the ordinary course of experience, even in the sciences, are hazardous in just this way. A single contrary instance is enough to refute them, and for the most part we have neither time nor capacity to examine every relevant instance. We accept a great many generalizations simply because our parents, teachers or other authorities have told us that they are true. Sometimes we adopt them by "wishful thinking"; we believe them because we want them to be true. Scientific inquiry, on the other hand, begins with an attitude of skepticism toward the pronouncements of authorities and the promptings of wishful thinking; it relies on a systematic observation of individual instances to support its generalizations. What constitutes adequate evidence for a scientific generalization? This question is the main problem for what is now usually called "inductive logic" or "scientific method". We shall not attempt to explore this question in detail in this book.

- 78 -

V. THE CATEGORICAL SYLLOGISM

1. Theory of the Syllogism

The logical inferences examined so far have all been "immediate" inferences in which a conclusion is drawn from a single premise. A syllogism, or "syllogistic" inference, is based on two separate premises. (If an argument has more than two premises, it is not called a syllogism, although the word 'syllogism' means simply "putting reasons together".) A categorical syllogism is one in which both of the premises, as well as the conclusion, are categorical propositions. There are several other types of syllogism which will be examined later.

In order to qualify as a categorical syllogism, an argument must not only contain exactly three categorical propositions (two premises and conclusion) but also these propositions must contain exactly three terms, each of which appears twice. For example,

> All dogs are domestic animals;
>
> All dachshunds are dogs;
>
> Hence, all dachshunds are domestic animals

satisfies these conditions. It is convenient to identify the various terms and premises by their traditional names. Thus

> The major term is the predicate of the conclusion ('domestic animals' is the example).
>
> The minor term is the subject of the conclusion (dachshunds').
>
> The middle term is the term common to both premises ('dogs').
>
> The major premise is the premise containing the major term (i.e., the first premise in the example).
>
> The minor premise is the premise containing the minor term.

Notice that the major and minor premises are defined by the fact that they contain the major or minor term, not by their position in the argument.

If we let 'S' represent the minor term, 'P' the major term and 'M' the middle term, the form of the syllogism given above appears as follows:

All M are P

All S are M

All S are P

or, in distribution shorthand,

Mp
$\underline{Sm}$
$\overline{Sp}$.

It seems pretty clear intuitively that this must be a valid argument. If every member of M is also a member of P, and if every member of S is one of the members of M, then (as the conclusion says) every S is a P. A formal proof of this result could easily be given in terms of our interpretation of quantified propositions. We know from the minor premise that

s_1 is an M

for example, so that for some particular member (m_i) of M

$s_1 = m_i$,

and we know also from the major premise that

m_i is a P,

from which it follows that

s_1 is a P;

and similar reasoning establishes similar results for the entire membership of S.

But there are many different forms of categorical syllogisms. They are traditionally classified according to "mood" and "figure". The mood of a syllogism is the specific pattern of propositional types (A, E, I, O) exhibited in its premises and conclusion. The example given is in the AAA mood, because its major premise, minor premise and conclusion

(in that order) are A-propositions. Since any of the
four propositional types can appear in each of these
three positions, we have 4^3 or 64 different possible
syllogistic moods. Moreover, each of these moods can
appear in any of four different configurations, or
figures, according to the positions of the terms in
the premises. Let us assume that all categorical
syllogisms are to be given in "standard form", i.e.,
with the major premise stated first and the minor premise second. Then the four possible figures, determined by the possible arrangements of terms, are:

```
    I        II     III       IV

  M - P    P - M   M - P     P - M

  S - M    S - M   M - S     M - S
```

Thus the example given above is in the first figure.
Taking account of the fact that each of the 64 moods
appears in four different figures, we see that there
are altogether 256 distinct forms of categorical
syllogism.

     So far we have established that one of these
forms, the AAA-mood in the first figure, is valid.
Several of the other forms can be shown to be valid
in a similar way, although the great majority cannot.
But it would be extremely tedious to examine each of
the remaining 255 forms in order to pick out the
valid ones. Instead of doing that here, we shall
simply list the results which an examination would
show as valid forms; then we shall discuss a method
for testing them. The valid forms of categorical
syllogism, listed by figure, are:

I	II	III	IV
AAA	AEE	AAI	AAI
AAI	AEO	AII	AEE
AII	AOO	EAO	AEO
EAE	EAE	EIO	EAO
EAO	EAO	IAI	EIO
EIO	EIO	OAO	IAI

     Now it happens that all of these 24 forms can

be shown to be valid if the six first-figure forms are valid, by a process known as "reduction." Moreover, we can derive all of the first-figure forms from just two of them: the AAA and the AII.

The latter syllogism,

All M are P   or: Mp
                                    sm
Some S are M   ──
                                    sp
───────────────
Some S are P

cannot be derived from the AAA syllogism but can be proved by an essentially similar argument. The minor premise asserts that at least one member (s_i) of S is a member of M, so that for some particular member (m_k) of M

$$s_i = m_k,$$

and since we know from the major premise that m_k must be a member of P, then so is s_i; this is enough to show that some S are P.

The second form (AAI) on the first-figure list is derived very simply from the AAA form by way of the subalternation rule in the square of opposition:

1. All M are P   hypothesis

2. All S are M   hypothesis
───────────────
3. All S are P   1, 2, AAA (AAA-syllog-
                             ism, first figure)

4. Some S are P   3, subalternation

The fifth form (EAO) is derived in exactly the same way from the fourth form (EAE). Syllogisms derived in this way, by subalternation from the conclusion of another syllogism, were called "weakened syllogisms" in traditional logic.

The remaining two forms in the first figure (EAE, EIO) can be derived with the help of our obversion rule. Thus we can derive EAE from AAA:

1.	No M are P	hypothesis
2.	All S are M	hypothesis

3.	All M are non-P	1, obversion
4.	All S are M	2, repetition (we can always repeat a step)
5.	All S are non-P	3, 4, AAA
6.	No S are P	5, obversion

And similarly we can derive EIO from AII

1.	No M are P	hypothesis
2.	Some S are M	hypothesis

3.	All M are non-P	1, obversion
4.	Some S are M	2, repetition
5.	Some S are non-P	3, 4, AII
6.	Some S are not P	5, obversion

Now by making use of conversion and other available operations of immediate inference we can "reduce" all of the valid forms in the other figures to those in the first figure. One example from each figure should suffice to show the method. For AEE in the second figure, we have

1.	All P are M	hypothesis
2.	No S are M	hypothesis

3.	No M are S	2, conversion
4.	All P are M	1, repetition
5.	No P are S	3, 4, EAE
6.	No S are P	5, conversion

For EAO in the third figure, we have

1.	No M are P	hypothesis

2.	All M are S	hypothesis

3.	No M are P	1, repetition
4.	Some S are M	2, conversion by limitation
5.	Some S are not P	3, 4, EIO

For IAI in the fourth figure, we have

1.	Some P are M	hypothesis
2.	All M are S	hypothesis

3.	Some P are M	1, repetition
4.	Some P are S	2, 3, AII
5.	Some S are P	4, conversion

Other cases of reduction are left to the reader.

If we have the complete list of valid syllogistic forms with us, when confronted by a syllogistic argument in every-day situations, we can simply compare the form of that argument with the forms on our list. But then we shall be frustrated if we have neglected to carry the list at all times. A slightly better method, perhaps, would be to memorize the list. Medieval logicians actually devised a Latin poem for this purpose. Each of the italicized names in the poem stands for a valid mood as indicated by the vowels in the name (e.g., Barbara for the AAA-mood). The first line mentions valid moods in the first figure ('prioris'), the second line the second figure ('secundae'), and so on. Even the consonants in the name are significant; they show how the various reductions are to be carried out, but we shall not pause to explore these refinements. The poem goes:

Barbara, Celarent, Darii, Ferioque, prioris;
Cesare, Camestres, Festino, Baroko, secundae;
Tertia, Darapti, Disamis, Datisi, Felapton,
Bokardo, Ferison, habet; Quarta insuper addit
Bramantip, Camenes, Dimaris, Fesapo, Fresison.

You will notice that not all of the valid forms are mentioned, but the omitted forms are all "weakened" syllogisms.

Those who find it difficult to memorize Latin poetry will find an alternative method in the next section.

EXERCISES

1. Write down each of the 24 valid forms of the categorical syllogism, using distribution short-hand. (These shorthand forms will be useful in connection with the material in the next section)

2. Identify the mood and figure of each of the following:

   a) All hippopotami are aquatic animals
      Some snakes are aquatic animals
      Hence, some snakes are hippopotami

   b) No parrots are pelicans
      No pelicans are peacocks
      Hence, no peacocks are parrots

   c) Some poems are epics
      Some poems are sonnets
      Hence, some sonnets are epics

   d) All Marxists are socialists
      Some politicians are not Marxists
      Hence, some politicians are not socialists

   e) All molecules are particles
      No particles are waves
      Hence, some waves are not molecules

2. Rules for Validity

A better way to test syllogistic arguments for validity would be to have a small set of easily re-membered rules. To be adequate for this purpose, this set of rules must be both necessary and sufficient to determine that any given categorical syllogism is valid or fallacious. It must be "necessary" in the sense that every valid form satisfies the rules, and it must be "sufficient" in the sense that every form that satisfies the rules is a valid form. Various sets of rules can be devised to meet these conditions. The set to be given here is generally regarded as con-venient and elegant.

There are two sorts of rules to be considered:
quality-rules (dealing with the affirmative or negative character of the proposition) and quantity-rules
(dealing with the distributed or undistributed character of the terms). We shall take these in order.

(A) Quality-rules.

1. No valid form has more than one
negative premise.

We can verify this rule quickly by inspecting our
table of the 24 valid forms. Clearly we never have
two E-propositions, two)-propositions or an E and an
O together as premises of a valid syllogistic form.
Hence this rule can be regarded as a necessary condition for validity of any syllogism.

2. If one premise is negative, the conclusion must be negative.

We can see that 16 of the valid forms have a
negative (E, O) premises, and there is a negative
conclusion in each case.

3. If no premise is negative, the conclusion must be affirmative.

This can be seen by inspecting the remaining eight
valid forms with affirmative premises.

(B) Quantity-rules.

1. Any middle term must be distributed at
least once.

At this point it will be helpful to consult the
results obtained in Exercise 1 at the end of the last
section. If you have represented the 24 forms correctly in distribution shorthand, you will see that the
middle term (M) is capitalized at least once in every
case (and sometimes twice).

2. Any term distributed in the conclusion
must also be distributed in the premises.

Again consulting the distribution shorthand, you
can see that every major (P) or minor (S) term capitalized in the conclusion is also capitalized in the major

or minor premise. Note that in some cases a major or minor term may be distributed in the premises without being distributed in the conclusion; this does not violate the rule.

Since each of these five rules is a necessary condition for the validity of a categorical syllogism, all of them must be satisfied by any valid argument in this form. This does not mean that every argument that fails to satisfy these rules must be fallacious; it might still be valid, but not a categorical syllogism as defined. For example, the argument that

No M are non-P

No S are non-M

Hence, all S are P

looks like a violation of the first quality-rule, having two negative premises. But the argument is obviously valid, since the premises are logically equivalent to the pair

All M are P

All S are M,

from which the same conclusion follows. In its original form, however, it is not a categorical syllogism, because it does not have exactly three terms.

We have not established that our five rules are sufficient as well as necessary conditions for validity; but the only way to do this is to show that no form other than the 24 valid forms satisfies them, and this would require inspecting all of the 232 remaining forms.

The various ways of violating the five rules can be discussed and identified more conveniently if we give them names, some of which are traditional.

We shall say that a syllogism violating the first quality-rule commits a <u>fallacy of two negatives</u>. For instance,

No diamonds are emeralds

Some diamonds are not vegetables

Hence, some vegetables are not emeralds

commits this fallacy because of its two negative premises. The propositions in this example are all true, of course, but this fact does not save the argument from being fallacious. Note that

No diamonds are organisms

Some diamonds are not vegetables

Hence, some vegetables are not organisms

has exactly the same logical form but is obviously fallacious because its conclusion is false while its premises are both true.

A syllogism violating the second quality-rule may be said to commit a fallacy of one negative, because it has an affirmative conclusion with one negative premise. For instance:

All professors are teachers

No monkeys are professors

Hence, all monkeys are teachers.

Note that the same premises do yield a valid conclusion, namely,

Some teachers are not monkeys,

which turns the argument into a valid EAO fourth figure syllogism. (Do you see why it is a fourth figure, not first figure, in the second version?)

A syllogism violating our third quality-rule is

All sharks are sea-creatures

All Hammerheads are sharks

Hence, some sea-creatures are not Hammerheads

which is really a transposed fourth figure. This may be called a fallacy of no negative, since the negative conclusion calls for a negative premise. Its fallacious character can be seen more clearly in the following example:

> All members of the species <u>homo sapiens</u>
> are people
>
> All human beings are members of the species
> <u>homo sapiens</u>
>
> Hence, some people are not human beings.

The proper conclusion, of course, would be

> All human beings are people. (What figure?)

In connection with the quantity-rules, consider:

> Some mammals are not porpoises
>
> All elephants are mammals
>
> Hence, no elephants are porpoises

where the middle term is not distributed in either premise. This is a <u>fallacy of undistributed middle</u>. The
fallacy shows itself more clearly if we substitute
'quadrupeds' for 'porpoises', which makes the conclusion false while the premises are true.

The second quantity-rule can be violated in
three different ways, depending on whether the minor
term, the major term, or both are at fault. In the
first case, we have a <u>fallacy of illicit minor</u>, e.g.,

> All huts are dwellings
>
> All dwellings are residences
>
> Hence, all residences are huts

where the minor term, 'residences', is illicitly distributed in the conclusion. On the other hand, in

> No bishops are mystics
>
> Some Christians are bishops
>
> Hence, no mystics are Christians

we have a <u>fallacy of illicit major</u>, because the term
"Christians' is illicitly distributed in the conclusion.
Both of these fallacies may occur in the same syllogism.

For example,

> Some planes are not bombers
>
> Some bombers are jets
>
> Hence, no jets are planes.

As you may have noticed, this rule concerning the distribution of terms in the conclusion of a syllogism is essentially the same as the rule against illicit promotions of terms in immediate inference (chapter 4).

We could shorten our list of rules, if desired, by combining the second and third quality-rules in a single rule:

> The conclusion is negative if and only if one premise is negative.

On the other hand, we shall see later that modern discoveries have led to certain changes in the theory of the syllogism, and in the revised version of the theory we shall not need to make use of the third quality-rule or the combined rule suggested above.

EXERCISES

Write down each of the following syllogistic arguments in distribution shorthand, identify the mood and figure, and name the fallacy (if any) in the argument. (Use the suggested letters to represent the terms in the shorthand.)

1. Some emperors are kings
    All emperors are male chauvinists
    Hence, all male chauvinists are kings   (E,K,M)

2. All banks are financial institutions
    Some financial institutions are pawn-shops
    Hence, some pawn-shops are banks   (B,F,P)

3. No pinochle-players are good bridge-
      players
    Some good bridge-players are not liars
    Hence, some pinochle-players are not
      liars   (P,B,L)

4. All ships are boats
   No ships are planes
   Hence, no planes are boats   (S,B,P)

5. All angels are celestial creatures
   No professors are angels
   Hence, some celestial creatures
   creatures are not professors   (A,C,P)

6. No valid arguments are unsound
      arguments
   Some legal briefs are valid arguments
   Hence, some legal briefs are unsound
      arguments   (V,U,L)

7. Some novels are not non-fiction
   All editorials are non-fiction
   Hence, some novels are not
      editorials   (N,F,E)

8. All carbon compounds are organic
      compounds
   All diamonds are organic compounds
   Hence, all diamonds are carbon
      compounds   (C,O,D)

9. All Freshpersons are Unitarians
   Some Freshpersons are Freshwomen
   Hence, all Freshwomen are
      Unitarians   (F,U,W)

10. No democracies are dictatorships
    Some democracies are military
       governments
    Hence, all dictatorships are
       military governments   (D,T,M)

3. Extensions of the theory

Often the following argument is given as an example of a syllogism:

All men are mortal

Socrates is a man

Hence, Socrates is mortal

But the theory of the categorical syllogism, as developed so far, does not seem to make room for this obviously valid argument. The argument is not in any of the recognized "moods" because two of its propositions are singulars rather than quantified propositions. The traditional solution to this problem was to treat singulars as special kinds of universals, on the theory that singular terms are really names of classes having just one member. From this point of view, we can interpret

Socrates is a man

as a way of saying

All members of the Socrates-class are men,

so that it can be handled as a universal affirmative for purposes of the syllogism. Likewise, we can interpret

Socrates is not a woman

as meaning

No members of the Socrates-class are women

which is a universal negative. This solution works well enough as long as we keep these single-member classes (unit classes, as they are now called) in the subject position. But if we have

No women are members of the Socrates-class

there is no corresponding singular proposition in the traditional sense.

Given this limitation, that singular terms can appear only as subject-terms, it is clear that only the minor premise of a categorical syllogism, not the major premise, can be a singular proposition, except in the third figure (where the middle term might be a singular term). For example,

Aristotle is a biologist

Aristotle is a philosopher

Hence, some philosophers are biologists,

is a valid third-figure syllogism. In the fourth

figure, where the minor term appears as predicate of the minor premise, there can be no singular propositions.

The theory of the syllogism can be extended in another way by developing certain consequences of the basic quality-rules and quantity-rules. These consequences take the form of derived rules, or theorems. Two of them, which we shall call Theorem II and Theorem III below, are often useful in practice and offer an interesting parallel to the quality-rules. It is easier to establish these results if we first establish a general rule concerning the number of distributed terms in any valid categorical syllogism.

Let us now call distributed terms 'D-terms' for short.

Theorem I. There must be at least one more D-term in the premises than in the conclusion.

Proof: by examining all possible cases, i.e., possible numbers of D-terms in a conclusion, showing that in each case there must be one additional D-term in the premises. Clearly there are just three cases: the conclusion may have no D-terms, one D-term or at most two D-terms.

Case 1: the conclusion has no D-term (and is therefore an I-proposition). In this case the premises must contain at least one D-term. Otherwise, the middle term is not distributed and we have a fallacy of undistributed middle.

Case 2: the conclusion has one D-term (and is therefore either an A-proposition or an O-proposition). Here there must be at least two D-terms in the premises, one of them being the middle term and the other being either the major or minor. Otherwise, we have either an undistributed middle or an illicit major or minor.

Case 3: the conclusion has two D-terms (and is thus an E-proposition). Here the premises must have three D-terms: one occurrence of the middle term, plus the major and minor terms.

Now we can make use of this theorem in deriving the following results.

Theorem II. No valid form has more than one

particular premise.

Proof by cases of possible pairs of particular premises.

Case 1:   both premises are I-propositions. Here there is no D-term in the premises, so we have a fallacy of undistributed middle.

Case 2: one premise is an I-proposition and the other is an O-proposition. In this case the conclusion should be negative (by the quality rules) and should have at least one D-term (its predicate). But then, by Theorem I, the premises should contain at least two D-terms. Since they only contain one D-term, the syllogism is not valid.

Case 3:   both premises are O-propositions. Here we have two negative premises, so the syllogism cannot be valid.

Theorem III.   If one premise is particular, the conclusion must be particular.

Proof by cases is left to the reader. There are four cases to consider; make use of Theorem I.

The validity of these three theorems can easily be verified by inspecting the list of valid syllogistic forms as represented in distribution shorthand.

In connection with syllogisms, confusion sometimes arises from a failure to distinguish valid arguments from sound arguments. In a valid argument, the conclusion must be true if the premises are true; but since in fact the premises may not be true, the conclusion may in fact be false. A sound argument is a valid argument having true premises; hence the conclusion of a sound argument is always true. For instance, the argument that

All men are human beings

Some men are infallible reasoners

Hence, some human beings are infallible
    reasoners

is formally valid (IAI in the third figure); but it is unsound because its major premise is not true -- or so most of us would say. There are no logical rules to

tell us, in general, what premises are true. A special
type of unsound syllogism often seen is the syllogism
with an ambiguous term, usually the middle term. For
example:

All fences are enclosures

All receivers of stolen goods are fences

Hence, all receivers of stolen goods are
enclosures.

This is a perfectly straight-forward case of AAA in the
first figure, and each of the premises is true in a
certain sense. But they are not true in the same sense,
because the middle term ('fences') has different meanings in the different premises. In the minor premise,
it has a figurative slang sense rather than the ordinary literal sense. Thus if we use the ordinary sense
the major premise is true but the minor is false, and
if we use the figurative sense the major is false but
the minor is true; in either case, the premises are
not both true. On the other hand, if we substitute
some other term (say, 'passer') for the figurative
occurrence of the term 'fence' we then have no categorical syllogism at all; it would have four terms.

EXERCISES

Prove Theorem III, as given in the text above.

4. Sorites

The conclusion of one syllogism can be used as
a premise for another, and in this way we can build up
a sort of chain-argument. Suppose we have

All penguins are birds

All birds are warm-blooded animals

Hence, all penguins are warm-blooded animals

and also

All penguins are warm-blooded animals
All warm-blooded animals are vertebrates

Hence, all penguins are vertebrates.

By suppressing the conclusion of the first argument and the minor premise of the second, and running the rest of it together, we obtain

All penguins are birds

All birds are warm-blooded animals

All warm-blooded animals are vertebrates

Hence, all penguins are vertebrates.

This is called a sorites (so-RY-teez), which is Greek for a "heap". In distribution shorthand, the example given has the form

Pb
Bw
Wv
$\overline{\text{Pv}}$

which also happens to be the <u>Aristotelian</u> <u>standard</u> <u>form</u> of the sorites.

A sorites can be made as long as you please, but of course, the longer ones are more tedious to analyze in terms of syllogisms. The analysis into syllogisms can be avoided if we can reduce the sorites to Aristotelian standard form. This means that (a) the first premise contains the minor term, (b) the last premise contains the major term, and (c) the intervening middle terms are arranged as shown in the example.

The basic rules for the categorical syllogism apply also to any form of sorites, namely:

A.1 No valid form has more than one negative premise

2. If one premise is negative, the conclusion must be negative

3. If no premise is negative, the conclusion must be affirmative

B.1. Any middle term must be distributed at least once

> 2. Any term distributed in the conclusion
> must also be distributed in the premises.

But in addition to these, there are two rules that apply specifically to the Aristotelian standard form sorites ('AS') namely:

> AS.1. If any premise is negative, it must be the last.

> AS.2. If any premise is particular, it must be the first.

The reason for the first rule is that any negative premise requires the conclusion to be negative, and if this negative premises is not the last (so that its predicate is the major term) we have an illicit major in the conclusion. The reason for the second rule is that any particular premise has an undistributed subject term, so that if it is any premise other than the first it leaves us with an undistributed middle somewhere.

It follows from these special rules that a sorites with a particular negative (O-proposition) premise cannot be put into Aristotelian standard form, although it may still be valid if it is composed of valid syllogisms. Sometimes this difficulty can be overcome by obverting the offending O-proposition, provided that its subject term is the minor term of the sorites. Otherwise, the argument can be analyzed by putting the remaining premises into Aristotelian form, drawing the appropriate conclusion from those premises and combining it with the O-premise to form a categorical syllogism.

That is about all there is to the theory of the sorites. Now for some examples.

Suppose we are given the argument

All politicians are crooks

All Assemblymen are legislators

All legislators are politicians   Pc

    Al

All crooks are criminals   Lp

    Cr

Hence, all Assemblymen are criminals   A̅r̅

We obtain a standard form sorites from this merely by

rearranging the premises thus:

All Assemblymen are legislators

All legislators are politicians

All politicians are crooks   Al

All crooks are criminals $\dfrac{\text{Lp}}{\text{Pc}}$

Hence, all Assemblymen are criminals $\dfrac{\text{Cr}}{\overline{\text{Ar}}}$

Often a simple rearrangement of premises is not enough, and we have to make use of obversion, conversion or both. For example:

All parallelograms are regular plane
  figures   Pf

All non-parallelograms are non-
  rectangles $\overline{\text{Pr}}$

No squares are non-rectangles $\text{S}\overline{\text{r}}$

Hence, all squares are regular plane
  figures. $\dfrac{}{\text{Sf}}$

To put this into standard form, we first put the premises in the right order:

No squares are non-rectangles $\text{S}\overline{\text{R}}$

All non-parallelograms are non-
  rectangles $\overline{\text{Pr}}$

All parallelograms are regular plane
  figures   Pf

Hence, all squares are regular plane
  figures. $\dfrac{}{\text{Sf}}$

Then by obverting the first premise and contraposing the second premise, we get

All squares are rectangles

All rectangles are parallelograms

All parallelograms are regular plane
  figures   Sr

Hence, all squares are regular plane
  figures, $\dfrac{\dfrac{\text{Rp}}{\text{Pf}}}{\overline{\text{Sf}}}$

which is in the desired standard form and is thus
clearly valid.

With a particular negative premise, however,
we may have a harder problem. Given that

All frescoes are paintings

Some works by Ghirlandaio are not allegories

All paintings are works of art

All works by Ghirlandaio are frescoes

Hence, some works of art are not
  allegories,

$$\begin{array}{c} Fp \\ gA \\ Pw \\ Gf \\ \hline wA \end{array}$$

we see that the second premise, an O-proposition, cannot be adapted to Aristotelian standard form because
its subject term is not the minor term (which is
'works of art'). Therefore, we first arrange the
other premises in standard form :

All works by Ghirlandaio are frescoes

All frescoes are paintings

All paintings are works of art,

which gives us the result that

All works by Ghirlandaio are works of art.

$$\begin{array}{c} Gf \\ Fp \\ Pw \\ \hline Gw \end{array}$$

Then we combine this result with the remaining premise
to obtain the syllogism

Some works by Ghirlandaio are not allegories

All works by Ghirlandaio are works of art

Hence, some works of art are not allegories,

which is a valid OAO syllogism, third figure.

An alternative standard form for the sorites is
the "Goclenian Standard Form", which looks like

$$\begin{array}{c} Ab \\ Ca \\ Dc \\ \hline Db \end{array}.$$

But since this form is really the same as the Aristotelian one with the premises in reverse order, it offers no new possibilities.

Rearrange the following arguments into Aristotelian standard form.

1. All scholars are learned people

    No persons subject to lapses of memory are infallible men

    No non-scholars are historians

    All learned people are persons subject to lapses of memory

    Hence, no historians are infallible men.

2. All fractions are ratios

    All non-fractions are integers

    All ratios are magnitudes

    Some numbers are not integers

    Hence, some numbers are magnitudes.

VI. NON-CATEGORICAL SYLLOGISMS AND TRUTH-FUNCTIONS

1. Compound Propositions

The forms of reasoning investigated up to this point have been those associated with the traditionally recognized "categorical" propositions, those propositions consisting in (or expressed by) simple indicative sentences. Naturally we have alluded to other sorts of propositions and even made use of them along the way, but without developing an explicit theory of them.

You will recall that we have been assuming that propositions can be regarded as indicative sentences, and it has been pointed out that from the grammatical point of view all sentences are simple, compound or complex. Hence one expects to find propositions that are compound and propositions that are complex in addition to the categorical propositions so far discussed. For purposes of traditional logical theory, however, we simplify matters by assuming that all non-categorical propositions are compound propositions. This is because we can always treat a complex sentence with subordinate clauses as an abbreviation for a compound sentence by transforming the subordinate clauses into co-ordinate clauses. Thus, given the complex sentence

> Napoleon, who had been defeated at Waterloo, was exiled to St. Helena.

we can rewrite it as a compound sentence, e.g.,

> Napoleon had been defeated at Waterloo, and he was exiled to St. Helena,

without any significant change in meaning or truth-value. A complex sentence without subordinate clauses, such as

> Napoleon thought that the time was ripe,

cannot be analyzed in the same way; but from the traditional point of view, at least, we can treat it as a categorical (singular) with an elaborate predicate term. Note that

> It is true that water is wet

is also a complex sentence, in that it contains the

sub-sentence

> Water is wet.

But in traditional logic both of these sentences were (implicitly) treated as categorical and equivalent propositions, just as

> It is false that grass is red

and

> Grass is not red

were treated as categorical and equivalent. For purposes of developing a modern theory of truth-functions, however, it is important to distinguish 'It is true that p' from 'p' and 'It is false that p' from 'q', where 'q' is the grammatically negative form of 'p'. From the modern point of view we should regard 'It is true that p' and 'It is false that p' as complex propositions rather than categorical ones.

Compound sentences are formed in natural languages in many different ways. But for logical purposes we shall assume that all of the different forms of compound sentences can be reduced to three basic forms: conjunctions, disjunctions and implications.   We have made use of these forms already in many places.

Given any pair of propositions (p, q, where 'q' may or may not be different from 'p'), we can form the conjunction

> (Both) p and q.

which is also a proposition. We can use or omit the initial word, 'both', as desired. In every-day discourse many other conjunctive words are used in place of 'and' (for example: 'but', 'although', 'in spite of the fact that', 'in addition to the fact that', 'even though', 'notwithstanding that'). The only function of these alternative words or phrases is to indicate some special interest in, or surprise at, the fact that both of the conjoined propositions are true. Thus we can interpret 'p, but q' as a way of saying something like 'p and q, and it is surprising that both p and q'. Sometimes, on the other hand, the word 'and' does not indicate a conjunction of the words or phrases surrounding it. For example, in

> Hitler was both crazy and clever

we do not have a "conjunction" of craziness with
cleverness. But we can interpret that sentence as
an abbreviation or ellipsis for

> Hitler was crazy, and Hitler was clever,

which is an ordinary conjunction. Or when we say
something like

> There are politicians, and there are
> politicians,

which looks like a (perfectly legitimate) conjunction of a proposition with itself, we usually mean
that

> There are politicians of one kind, and
> there are politicians of another kind,

which is a conjunction of two different propositions.

We can also form the disjunction

> (Either) p or q

of any two propositions, or of any proposition with
itself. In logical theory we find it convenient to
use the disjunctive word 'or' in a rather special
sense, in which it means that at least one (and
possibly both) of the two propositions joined by it
is true. This use corresponds to the phrase 'and/or',
which appears often in business-English. In standard
English, 'or' tends to mean that only one (and not
both) of the propositions is true. For logical purposes, we can construct this standard sense by writing

> p or q, and not both p and q,

where 'not both p and q' means 'it is false that both
p and q'.

Finally, we can form the implication (or
conditional)

> If p, (then) q

from any two propositions, or from any proposition and
itself. Often this appears in the form

        q, if p

or

        p only if q,

which means the same thing. In an implication, the
first proposition (p) is the antecedent of the implication, and the second proposition (q) is the
consequent. (The same terminology can be applied to
conjunctions and disjunctions.) It is important to
remember this distinction, since obviously the proposition

        If q then p

or, equivalently,

        p if q

or

        q only if p,

is quite different from the first example and does
not necessarily have the same truth-value. Notice
that in the '...only if...' form, the proposition
following 'if' is the consequent of the implication,
not the antecedent. This is apt to cause some confusion. It might be helpful to think of 'p only if q'
as an ellipsis for

        Not p, if not q,

which clearly means

        If not q then not p;

and we shall see later that this proposition is
equivalent to 'If p then q'.

        A special caution must be noted concerning the
phrase 'provided that', which is ambiguous. When I
say, "You will graduate provided that you pass English Comp," you will probably understand me to be
saying that you will graduate if you pass English
Comp; but I might be intending to say that you will
graduate only if you pass English Comp. Ordinary
usage does not seem to have settled decisively on
one or the other of these interpretations.

Another important type of compound proposition is the _equivalence_ (or biconditional):

       p if and only if q.

But we do not need to treat this as one of our basic types, because we can interpret it in terms of those already defined. It is an abbreviation for

       p if q, and p only if q,

or, in other words,

       If q then p, and if p then q

or equivalently

       If p then q, and if q then p.

The propostions joined by conjunction, disjunction or implication may themselves be simple (categorical), complex or compound. In the example given immediately above, we have a conjunction of two implications. That is, the proposition as a whole is in the form of a conjunction ('(Both)... and ...'); but its antecedent ('if p then q') is an implication, and its consequent ('if q then p') is an implication. In another example mentioned earlier,

       p or q, and not both p and q,

we have a conjunction in which the antecedent ('p or q') is a disjunction and the consequent ('not both p and q') is the negation of a conjunction. In fact, the consequent in this case is itself complex, since it contains the conjunction 'both p and q' as a component. Clearly there is no limit to the degree of complexity that these non-categorical propositions might exhibit. As this degree increases, it may become increasingly difficult to sort out what is actually being asserted; and in the long run it is necessary to devise some sort of shorthand or symbolism, like that of mathematics, to make complicated statements more perspicuous and manageable. Arithmetic could not have advanced very far if we had no shorthand way of representing such a statement as, for example:

       The ratio of the product of two and three to four is equal to the ratio of three to two.

This takes the relatively simple form

$$(2 \times 3)/4 = 3/2$$

which we learn in elementary school and which seems much clearer to us than the verbal statement, although it is merely a shorthand representation for that statement.

The idea of constructing a logical symbolism comparable to the symbolisms of arithmetic and algebra now seems very obvious, but it did not occur to anyone until quite late in the history of Western thought. Descartes and Spinoza first suggested that mathematical proof-methods could be applied to philosophical reasoning of all sorts, and some of their works (notably Spinoza's Ethics) actually imitate the form of geometrical treatises, although they made no attempt to introduce logical symbols. The concept of a quasi-algebraic symbolism for logic was discussed by Leibniz (1646-1716), but he made only very tentative explorations in that direction. The first really successful formulations of what we now know as "symbolic logic" occurred in the mid-nineteenth century in the work of Augustus De Morgan (1806-71), George Boole (1815-64) and, most especially, the American philosopher Charles Peirce (1839-1914). Although we will not be able to explore these developments in great detail, we will see later how the use of certain special symbols makes the analysis of complicated propositions and arguments easier.

EXERCISES

Decide whether the following sentences express categorical or non-categorical propositions; in the latter case, identify their general forms (conjunction, disjunction, implication) and the forms of their components (antecedent and consequent).

1. Kennedy and Johnson both took a firm stand against Russian expansionism.

2. Mrs. Wiggins decided to buy either a turkey or a ham.

3. Neither George Eliot nor George Sand was a male, but both were successful novelists.

4. Johnny will succeed if he doesn't waste his time playing poker.

5. If you are 65 years of age or older, or blind in both eyes, you may claim one extra exemption.

2. Traditional Forms of Inference

The simpler forms of compound propositions were known in ancient times, and most of the basic forms of inference involving such propositions were investigated by the Stoics.

The traditionally recognized inferences chiefly concern implications and disjunctions. Arguments involving conjunctions were not explicitly recognized, perhaps because the properties of conjunction itself seems so obvious intuitively that we are constantly making use of conjunctive arguments without being aware of it. For example, it seems obvious that if we know that

1. The barn door is open

and

2. The horse is gone,

then it follows that

3. The barn door is open, and the horse is gone.

And conversely, if

1. The barn door is open, and the horse is gone

then clearly

2. The barn door is open,

and clearly also

3. The horse is gone,

But we make these inferences so rapidly and automatically that we hardly feel them as inferences at all.

Three of the traditional forms make use of an implication in combination with another implication or

with the affirmation or negation of its own antecedent
or consequent; the others make use of a disjunction in
combination with the ngeation of its antecedent or
consequent or with implications. We shall begin with
the former group.

     1. <u>Modus ponens</u> (also called 'affirming the
antecedent'). In this form of argument, one premise
is an implication and the other premise is the antecedent of the implication; the conclusion is that the
consequent is true. Thus:

    If it rains, then it pours.

    It rains.

    Hence, it pours.

More generally, then

    If p then q

$$\frac{p}{q}$$

Of all forms of logical inference, this is perhaps the
most widely used and the most generally acknowledged
as valid. Its name, 'modus ponens', is short for
'modus ponendo ponens', the "method of affirming by
affirming", so called because it reaches an affirmative
conclusion by affirming one of the components of a compound proposition. But the component that is affirmed
must be the antecedent, not the consequent. An argument like

    If the witness is guilty, he pleads the fifth
     Amendment.

    He pleads the fifth Amendment.

    Hence, the witness is guilty

is <u>not</u> valid; it commits the fallacy of "affirming the
consequent". If this sort of reasoning were valid, it
would mean in effect that the first premise ('If the
witness is guilty, he pleads the fifth Amendment') has
exactly the same logical force as its converse,

    If he pleads the fifth Amendment, the witness
     is guilty,

which is contrary to our understanding of the use of
implication statements. We need to allow for the
possibility that the latter implication is false even
though the former is true; and this is the same as
the possibility that its consequent ('the witness is
guilty') is false even though its antecedent ('he
pleads the fifth Amendment') is true.

   2. Modus tollens (or "denying the consequent").
In this argument, one premise is the negation of the
consequent of the other premise, which is an implication. For example:

> If today is Tuesday, we're in Belgium.
>
> We're not in Belgium.
>
> Hence, today is not Tuesday.

This has the general form

> If p then q
>
> Not q
> _____
>
> Not p

The name 'modus tollens' is short for 'modus tollendo
tollens', the "method of denying by denying". This
sort of reasoning is very useful in connection with
the experimental sciences, or for that matter any
theoretical discipline, where in order to make pro-
gress one must show that some previously accepted
theory (p) is false by showing that it implies some
false consequence (q).

   Arguments which look like modus tollens but depend on denying the antecedent, instead of the consequent, like

> If John is a Freshman, than John is a
>   student.
>
> John is not a Freshman.
>
> Hence, John is not a student,

are not valid; they commit the fallacy of "denying the
antecedent". The objection to reasoning of this type
is essentially the same as the objection to "affirming
the consequent".

3. **Hypothetical syllogism** (or "transitivity of implication"). In this form we have two implication-premises, such that the antecedent of one is the consequent of the other. For example:

> If she makes a good impression, she gets the job.
>
> If she gets the job, she can afford a car.
>
> Hence, if she makes a good impression, she can afford a car.

The general form is

> If p then q
>
> If q then r
> _____
> if p then r

There is a certain formal analogy between this argument and the categorical syllogism, especially the AAA mood in the fourth figure (or first figure, if we reverse the order of the premises). This analogy is not accidental, as we shall see later, and in fact it is always possible to translate categorical syllogisms into hypothetical ones.

4. **Disjunctive syllogism** (or "modus tollendo ponens"). Here one premise is a disjunction, and the other is the negation of one of its components. For example:

> Either the Israelis will make concessions, or the Arabs will strike again
>
> The Israelis will not make concessions.
>
> Hence, the Arabs will strike again,

with the general form

> Either p or q
>
> Not p
> _____
> q

Since disjunctions are symmetrical ('p or q' being
equivalent to 'q or p'), it is clear that

> Either q or p
>
> Not p
>
> ———————————
>
> q

is also a valid argument, and it goes by the same
name. The traditional Latin name, 'modus tollendo
ponens', means "method of affirming by denying".

Notice, however, that we do not get a valid argument by affirming one of the components of a disjunction. Thus,

> Either p or q
>
> p
>
> ———————————
>
> Not q

is not valid, and is called a fallacy of "affirming
a disjunct". The reason is that in logical theory we
assume that both components of a disjunction may be
true if the disjunction itself is true. On the other
hand,

> Either not p or not q
>
> p
>
> ———————————
>
> Not q

is a valid argument, and is an instance of the disjunctive syllogism, if we assume that 'p' is logically
equivalent to "not not p".

5. The dilemma (meaning "two lemmas" or "two
branches"). Here we have a disjunction plus two implications, as in the following example:

> Either Congress defeats the education
>   bill, or the President vetoes it.
>
> If Congress defeats the education bill,
>   there will be no fellowships

If the President vetoes it, there will
be no fellowships.

Hence, there will be no fellowships.

There are four different forms of dilemma. This one
has the form

Either p or q

if p then r

if q then r

_____

r

It is called a "simple constructive dilemma"; "simple,"
because the two implication-premises have the same
consequent, and "constructive" because the conclusion
affirms that porposition. In a "complex constructive
dilemma" the two implications have different consequents, and the conclusion affirms their disjunction.
For instance:

Either men love you or the gods favor you.

If men love you, you are famous.

If the gods favor you, you are fortunate.

Hence, either you are famous or you are
fortunate.

This has the form

Either p or q

If p then r

If q then s

_____

Either r or s

In a "simple destructive dilemma" the components of
the disjunction are negative, the two implications
have a common antecedent, and the conclusion is the
negation of that antecedent. For example:

Either Lenin did not believe in the
"withering away" of the state, or he
did not think the time was ripe.

If Lenin was a Marxist, Lenin did believe
in the "withering away" of the state.

If Lenin was a Marxist, he did think
the time was ripe.

Hence, Lenin was not a Marxist.

The general form is

Either not p or not q

If r then p

If r then q

_____

Not r

Finally, the "complex destructive dilemma" differs from
the preceding one in that the two implications have
different antecedents and the conclusion is a disjunction of the negations of those antecedents. For example:

Either she doesn't love me or she isn't
serious about the other guy.

If she's angry at me, she loves me.

If she has forgotten me, she is serious
about the other guy.

Hence, either she's not angry with me, or
she has not forgotten me.

The general form is

Either not p or not q

If r then p

If s then q

_____

Either not r or not s

As the reader may have noticed, we could vary these
"destructive" forms by having the negation of 'p' or
the negation of 'q', or both, appear in the implication-
premises rather than the disjunction; the same conclusions would then follow.

6. <u>Reductio</u> <u>ad</u> <u>absurdum</u> ("leading to absurdity").
This method of reasoning consists in showing that some
given hypothesis leads to contradictory results and is
therefore false. <u>Reductio</u> was so dear to classical
mathematicians that they did not regard a theorem of
geometry or arithmetic as fully established unless it
had been proved by this method. We can represent it
as a pair of implication-premises with a common antecedent and with contradictory consequents, and with
the negation of the antecedent as conclusion. For
example:

> If some ratio of integers equals the root
> of 2, it has an even denominator.
>
> If some ratio of integers equals the root
> of 2, it does not have an even denominator.
>
> Hence, no ratio of integers equals the
> root of 2.

The general form is

> If p then q
>
> If p then not q
>
> _____
>
> Not p

A slight variation of this form is **indirect proof**,
where the common antecedent is the negation of some
proposition which the conclusion affirms:

> If not p then q
>
> If not p then not q
>
> _____
>
> p

This form is easily derived from the <u>reductio</u> form
if we assume that 'p' is equivalent to 'not not p'.
The reductio form itself can be regarded as a special
case of the simple destructive dilemma, in which the
disjunctive premise has been tacitly assumed:

Either not q or not not q

If p then q

If p then not q

_____

Not p

EXERCISES

State the general form of each of the following arguments, and assess their validity.

1. If God is willing but unable to prevent evil, He is impotent. If God is able but unwilling to prevent evil, He is malevolent. But either He is not impotent or He is not malevolent. Therefore, either God is not willing but unable to prevent evil, or God is not able but unwilling to prevent evil.

2. If we buy the TV set, we can't afford the dishwasher. But we are not buying the TV set. Therefore, we can afford the dishwasher.

3. Either you pass Freshman Comp or you don't get your degree. You have passed Freshman Comp. Hence, you do get your degree.

4. This couple will be admitted only if they have tickets. But they do not have tickets. Therefore, this couple will not be admitted.

5. Bobby is a success if the girls like him. Unfortunately, the girls do not like him. Hence, Bobby is not a success.

6. Either new oil deposits are going to be found soon, or there will be shortages. New oil desposits are not going to be found soon. So there will be shortages.

7. Mr. Smith has gone and bought himself a horse. But if Mr. Smith has gone and bought himself a horse, there must be a good reason for it. Hence, there must be a good reason for it.

8. This method works if it is tried and true. But this method doesn't work. Therefore, it is not tried and true.

3. Truth-functions

In the last section, we examined the basic forms of argument in which conjunctions, disjunctions and implications appear as premises. Now we shall determine under what conditions these compound propositions are true or false. In doing so, we take advantage of the fact that they are truth-functional propositions ("truth-functions" for short).

A truth-function is a compound or complex proposition whose truth-value is determined by the truth-values of its components. Many compound or complex propositions are non-truth functional. For instance,

> Jefferson wrote that all mean are created equal

is evidently not truth-functional, because its truth-value does not seem to depend in any way on the truth or untruth of the proposition that all men are created equal. On the other hand, a singular negative proposition, such as

> Chief Justice Marshall was not a Yankee,

is truth-functional, because we take it to mean that

> It is false that Chief Justice Marshall was a Yankee

and this proposition is clearly true if

Chief Justice Marshall was a Yankee

is false, and it is false if the latter proposition
is true.

More generally, the negation of any proposition
('p') always has the opposite truth-value, if we
assume that we have just two such values. Hence,

If 'p' is true, then 'Not p' is false; and

if 'p' is false, then 'not 'p' is true.

This pair of implicational rules completely determines
the functional relationships between the values of
'p' and 'not p'. Notice that it follows from these
rules that if 'not p' is true then 'p' is false, and
that if 'not p' is false then 'p' is true. For
suppose the contrary: i.e., suppose that 'not p' is
true but still 'p' is not false. If 'p' is not false,
then it is true; and if it is true, then (by the first
rule) 'not p' is false. But then 'not p' is both
true and false, which is absurd. Or suppose that
'not p' is false but still 'p' is not true; then again
the same absurdity results.

A convenient and widely used method for representing these truth-functional relationships is the
truth-table. A truth-table is simply a shorthand
way to display the information contained in truth-
functional rules like those we have just considered.
It consists of two or more columns and two or more
rows: one or more columns of values for the components of the complex or compound proposition to be
analyzed, and one column for the corresponding values
of that proposition; two or more rows of values,
corresponding to the number of possible values
assignable to the components. The truth-table for
negation is:

p	not p
true	false
false	true

Usually, this table is given in the more compact form

p	not p
T	F
F	T

or, if we use '1' to stand for 'true' and '0' for 'false',

p	not p
1	0
0	1

This last form, which is easy to read and easily extended to logical systems with more than two truth-values, will be adopted in what follows.

The tables for conjunction, disjunction and implication are more elaborate, because each of these types of proposition has two components (antecedent and consequent). But the principle is the same, namely that the table represents the information contained in the set of implicational rules that spell out the basic truth-functional relationships. In the case of conjunction, as we have seen, these relationships are very obvious. A conjunction is true if and only if both of its components are true. Hence:

If both 'p' is true and 'q' is true, then 'both p and q' is true;

if both 'p' is true and 'q' is false, then 'both p and q' is false;

if both 'p' is false and 'q' is true, then 'both p and q' is false;

if both 'p' is false and 'q' is false, then 'both p and q' is false.

This gives the corresponding truth-table:

p	q	both p and q
1	1	1
1	0	0
0	1	0
0	0	0

Note how the table shows that if a conjunction is true then both of its components are true, although it does not explicitly contain that information. If a conjunction were true while one or more of its components were false, then (by rows 2, 3 and 4 of the table) the conjunction would also be false, which is absurd.

In the case of disjunction, we need only bear in mind that we want to interpret 'p or q' as meaning "p and/or q" rather than "either p or q, but not both". In other words, a disjunction will be true if its antecedent, its consequent, or both, is true. Hence:

If both 'p' is true and 'q' is true, then 'either p or q' is true;

if both 'p' is true and 'q' is false, then 'either p or q' is true;

if both 'p' is false and 'q' is true, then 'either p or q' is true;

if both 'p' is false and 'q' is false, then 'either p or q' is false.

The truth-table therefore is:

p	q	either p or q
1	1	1
1	0	1
0	1	1
0	0	0

Note that the table shows that if a disjunction is false then both its components are false. It also illustrates the validity of the traditional disjunctive syllogism.

For we can see in row three, which is the only row in which 'either p or q' is true while 'p' is false, that 'q' (the conclusion of the syllogism) is true; similarly, the second row shows that 'p' is true if 'either p or q' is true while 'q' is false.

The case of implication presents more difficulty, because at first sight it is not clear that an implication is truth-functional at all. For instance, it seems to be true that

If the defendant committed murder, then he committed homicide, which follows from the way we use the term 'murder'; and this implication seems to be true whether the defendant actually committed murder or not, and whether he actually committed homicide or not. If so, its truth-value is quite independent of the values of its components. Similarly, its converse, that

If the defendant committed homicide, then he committed murder, seems to be false regardless of the values of its components. Nevertheless, a closer look reveals that these implications are just as truth-functional as the other types of compound propositions we have examined. For suppose that 'the defendant committed murder' is true while 'the defendant committed homicide' is false, which is one of the possible configurations of values to be considered. In that case, the statement 'If the defendant committed murder, then he committed homicide' must be false; otherwise, if it were true, then by the rule of modus ponens it would follow that the defendant committed homicide, which was assumed to be false.

In other words, we would have the following proof:

1. The defendant committed murder, and he did not commit homicide.   (hypothesis)

2. If the defendant committed murder, then he committed homicide.   (hypothesis)

---

3. The defendant committed murder. (by step 1)

4. He committed homicide.   (2, 3, modus ponens)

5. He did not commit homicide.   (by step 1)

Since the last two steps are contradictory, the two hypotheses cannot both be true, given that the rule of modus ponens and the truth-table for conjunction are valid. Hence we have, in effect, one row of a truth-table for implication:

If both 'p' is true and 'q' is false, then 'If p then q' is false,

or

p	q	If p then q
1	1	?
1	0	0
0	1	?
0	0	?

It remains to be shown that an implication is true in all cases except the one just mentioned, where its antecedent is true and its consequent is false.

(1) Suppose that 'p' and 'q' are both true. If the implication were false in this case, it would be false whenever 'p' were true; for we already know that it is false in the second row, the only other case where 'p' is true. Consequently, when 'if p then q' was true, 'p' would be false whether 'q' were true or not. But then from the pair of premises

If p then q

q

we could infer that 'p' is false, which is a fallacy of affirming the consequent. Hence we must conclude that

If both 'p' is true and 'q' is false, then 'If p then q' is true,

or

p	q	If p then q
1	1	1
1	0	0
0	1	?
0	0	?

(2)   Suppose that 'p' and 'q' are both false.
Then if the implication is false, it will be false
whenever 'q' is false, whether 'p' is true or not;
for we already know that it is false in the second
row, the only other case where 'q' is false. Consequently, whenever 'If p then q' is true, so is
'q'; and then we ought to be able to infer 'q' from
the pair of premises

        If p then q

        Not p.

But this is a fallacy of denying the antecedent.
Hence

        If both 'p' is false and 'q' is false,
        then "if p then q' is true,

or

p	q	If p then q
1	1	1
1	0	0
0	1	?
0	0	1

    (3)   Suppose finally that 'p' is false and 'q' is
true.   Then if the implication is false, it will be
false whenever 'p' and 'q' have different truth-values.
Consequently, whenever 'If p then q' is true, 'p' and
'q' are both true or both false.   But this would permit both of the fallacies already mentioned, affirming
the consequent and denying the antecedent.   Hence

        If both 'p' is false and 'q' is true, then
'If p then q' is true, so that the completed truth-
table for implication is

p	q	If p then q
1	1	1
1	0	0
0	1	1
0	0	1

Note how this differs from the truth-table for the converse proposition, 'If q then p':

p	q	If q then p
1	1	1
1	0	1
0	1	0
0	0	1

This difference results from the non-symmetrical character of implications. Unlike conjunctions and disjunctions, implications are not logically equivalent to their converses. Otherwise, the fallacies we have noted would not be fallacies.

Our basic repertoire of truth-tables is now complete. Before proceeding further, it will be convenient to introduce a little shorthand.

The rather cumbersome phrases, 'both...and...', 'either...or...', 'if...then...', and so forth, are ways of indicating various relations between pairs of propositions. Usually we can drop one or another of the words in these phrases without difficulty and with some gain in economy. For example,

instead of	we might have	or perhaps
both p and q	p and q	both: p, q
either p or q	p or q	either: p, q
if p then q	p then q	if p, q

(or: p only if q)

These alternative strategies for abbreviation suggest two alternative kinds of shorthand notation for representing truth-functional compound propositions. One kind of shorthand replaces the connective words 'and', 'or' and 'then' with special symbols; the other kind replaces the introductory words 'both', 'either' and 'if'. In both kinds, the negation of a proposition (p), 'not p', is represented by placing a special symbol for negation immediately in front of the proposition. Among the many different systems of symbols currently used, we shall find the so-called Polish

notation most convenient here. According to this
system, we represent

negation   by 'N'

conjunction   by 'K'

disjunction   by 'A'

implication   by 'C'.

Hence we can replace

not p   by   Np

both p and q   by   p K q   or by   Kpq

either p and q by   p A q   or by   Apq

if p then q   by   p C q   or by   Cpq.

According to the first method, which is more widely
used, the truth-functional connective symbols are
infix operators placed between the two components of
the compound expression. If this expression is to
be part of some larger compound, it must be set off
by parentheses, brackets or braces. Thus, to form
the negation of a conjunction 'p K q' we would have
to write

N(p K q),

which is clearly a different proposition from

Np K q,

the conjunction of the negation of "p" with "q".
According to the other method, the connectives are
treated as prefix operators. This method has the
advantage of not requiring parentheses. Thus the
negation of a conjunction 'Kpq' is simply

NKpq,

while the conjunction of the negation of its antecedent (p) with its consequent (q) is

KNpq.

    In practice, the Polish-notation symbols are
normally used as prefix operators, and when infix

operators are used they are more apt to be special non-alphabetic symbols like the following:

a dash ('__') or tilde ('~') for negation

a dot ('.') or ampersand ('&') for conjunction

a wedge ('v' or 'V') for disjunction (suggested by the Latin 'vel')

a horseshoe ('⊃') or arrow ('→') for implication.

But in principle any of these different sorts of symbols can be used either way, as infix operators or prefix operators.

Some of the advantages and disadvantages in each method can be seen when we apply them to some examples previously discussed. To represent 'Either p or q, and not both p and q', we have either

(p A q) K N(p K q)   or   KApqNKpq.

For 'p if and only if q', or in other words 'if p then q, and if q then p', we have either

(p C q) K (q C p)   or   KCpqCqp.

For the traditional rule of modus ponens,

If p then q

p

_____

q

we now have either

p C q   or   Cpq

p   p

_____   ___

q   q

and similar shorthand for the other rules of inference. Since both methods are just alternative ways of saying exactly the same things, the choice is a matter of taste and convenience. For very long and complicated compounds, the infix method perhaps shows their logical forms more clearly, but on the other hand the prefix

method saves a good deal of space. Thus, for 'if
both p and either q or r, then either both p and q
or both p and r' we can choose between

  (p K (q A r)) C ((p K q) A (p K r))

and

  CKpAqrAKpqKpr.

Since there are times when clarity of form is more
important than compactness, and other times when
compactness is more important than clarity of form,
we have good reason to cultivate both methods and
not discard one in favor of the other.

                    EXERCISES

Symbolize each of the following (a) using infix
operators and (b) using prefix operators.

   1. Neither if p then q nor if p then p (i.e.,
       Not either...or...).

   2. If both not r and if s then r, then not s.

   3. If if either s or t then q, then both if s
       then q and if t then q.

   4. If either q or r, then not either not q or
       not r.

   5. If either p or both q and r, then both
       either p or q and either p or r.

4. Applications of Truth-Tables

   The method of truth-tables can be extended so as
to cover all compound propositions constructed out
of conjunctions, disjunctions, implications and their
possible combinations. In this way it becomes an
important aid in the evaluation of certain kinds of
arguments. It also gives rise to some rather surprising results, as will be seen.

   The simplest extension of the truth-table method
occurs in connection with the concept of negation.
As our basic table for negation shows, the negation

('Np') of any proposition ('p') always has a value
different from the value of the proposition itself:

p	Np
1	0
0	1

Since this relation must hold no matter what specific content is given to 'p', we also have, for example,

Kpq	NKpq
1	0
0	1

Once we have established a basic column of values for
the conjunction 'Kpq', therefore, we can easily construct a column of values for its negation 'NKpq' by
extending the truth-table for the conjunction itself:

p	q	Kpq	NKpq
1	1	1	0
1	0	0	1
0	1	0	1
0	0	0	1

Obviously the same method applies to every truth-
functional compound. The values for the negation of
the compound will always differ in each row from the
corresponding value of the compound itself. Thus for
disjunction we have

p	q	Apq	NApq
1	1	1	0
1	0	1	0
0	1	1	0
0	0	0	1

and for implication we have

p	q	Cpq	NCpq
1	1	1	0
1	0	0	1
0	1	1	0
0	0	1	0

Similar extensions of the truth-table occur in connection with conjunction, disjunction and implication. Consider, for example, the concept of equivalence: 'p if and only if q'. We have already defined this relation as meaning 'if p then q, and if q then p', a conjunction of two implications. Since the columns of values for these implications are established, we can construct a column of values for their conjunction by applying the table for conjunction. In other words, where both implications have the value of '1', their conjunction will also have '1'' otherwise, it will have '0'. This gives the result:

p	q	Cpq	Cqp	KCpqCqp
1	1	1	1	1
1	0	0	1	0
0	1	1	0	0
0	0	1	1	1

To represent the concept of equivalence more briefly, we can use the special symbol 'E' and write

'Epq' as an abbreviation for 'KCpqCqp'

or, with infix notation,

'p E q' as an abbreviation for '(p C q) K (q C p)'.

Consider also what may be called the concept of exclusive disjunction: 'either p or q, and not both p and q'. Clearly we can construct a truth-table for this relation by the same method, since it too is a conjunction of two compounds for which we have established columns of values. In this case we have:

p	q	Kpq	Apq	NKpq	KApqNkpq
1	1	1	1	0	0
1	0	0	1	1	1
0	1	0	1	1	1
0	0	0	0	1	0

This result is interesting because of its close relationship to the table previously established for
equivalence. If we now compute the values for the
negation of an equivalence (let us say 'non-equivalence' for short),

Epq	NEpq
1	0
0	1
0	1
1	0

we see that the column for non-equivalence is exactly
the same as the column for exclusive disjunction.
This means that the two propositions in question,
'NEpq' and 'KApqNKpq' must themselves be equivalent;
they will always have the same truth-value. We could
now represent this equivalence explicitly in our notation by writing

ENEpqKApqNKpq

or, with infix operators,

N(p E q) E ((p A q) K N(p K q)),

and we can construct a truth-table column for this
expression also. If we do so, we get:

NEpq	KApqNKpq	ENEpqKApqNKpq
0	0	1
1	1	1
1	1	1
0	0	1

As the last column shows, the equivalence is true
in every possible case, no matter what values are
assigned to its ultimate components (p, q). Propositions of this kind are called tautologies. If we
assume that our truth-tables are adequate representations of valid rules of inference in our logic, then
clearly whatever the table indicates to be true in
every possible case must be provable in the logic;
and indeed the truth-table itself can be taken as a
proof. Thus every tautology is a theorem, and, if
the logic is valid, is a logical truth or necessarily
true proposition. But not every theorem or logical
truth is a tautology; for the concept of tautology
applies only to the truth-functional part of logical
theory and does not apply, for example, to the theory
of immediate inference or the categorical syllogism.

A few elementary tautologies, which are of special
interest for logical theory and philosophy, are functions of a single variable ('p'). These are the law
of excluded middle ('ApNp'), the law of non-contradiction ('NKpNp'), the reflexivity of implication ('Cpp')
and the reflexivity of equivalence ('Epp'). Traditionally, these were often identified as the most
fundamental "laws of thought", although in modern times
the first two have been subject to controversy. The
reader can verify them easily by truth-tables.

Another important group of tautologies concerns
the relations between conjunctions and disjunctions.
Off hand, there seems to be no particularly interesting similarity between conjunctions and disjunctions.
But if we look at the truth-table column for the negation of a conjunction, 'NKpq', and compare it to the
column for the disjunction 'Apq', we have

NKpq	Apq
0	1
1	1
1	1
1	0

where each column is exactly like the other column
upside down. This reversal of the order of values in
a column is what would happen if the values of the
variables (p, q) were stated in the reverse order, or
-- what amounts to the same thing -- if the negations

of those variables were used in place of their affirmative forms. This conjecture is confirmed by the table
below:

p	q	Np	Nq	ANpNq
1	1	0	0	0
1	0	0	1	1
0	1	1	0	1
0	0	1	1	1

Since the column for ''ANpNq' is the same as the column
for 'NKpq', these two propositions are equivalent, and
their equivalence ('EANpNqNKpq') can be established as
a tautology. Thus the negation of a conjunction is
equivalent to the disjunction of the negations of its
components. As intuition suggests, it also turns out
that the negation of a disjunction is equivalent to
the conjunction of the negations of its components;
the proof is left to the reader as an exercise. This
pair of equivalences (together with some related results) is called "De Morgan's Theorem" in honor of the
English logician and mathematician Augustus De Morgan,
who discovered the basic principle involved.

If we can establish theorems in our logic by way
of truth-tables, by the same token we can establish
the validity of complicated truth-functional arguments.
Certain classical argument-forms have been taken as
the basis for the truth-tables themselves. If these
arguments are written out in the form of implication-
statements (rather than as vertically ordered proof-
schemas), the implication-statements always turn out
to be tautologies. The rule of modus ponens, for
instance,

Cpq

p
___

q

can be put in the form of an implication in which the
conjunction of the premises ('Cpq', 'p') appears as
antecedent and the conclusion ('q') appears as consequent:

CKCpqpq

or, with infix notation,

$$((p \subset q) \; K \; p) \subset q.$$

The truth-table for this implication

p	q	Cpq	KCpqp	CKCpqpq
1	1	1	1	1
1	0	0	0	1
0	1	1	0	1
0	0	1	0	1

reveals it as a tautology. Similar results are obtained for all of the classical valid argument-forms.
Indeed, it is not difficult to show that <u>any</u> valid
truth-functional argument must correspond to some
tautological implication. The validity of an argument is reflected in the truth-table by the fact that
whenever a '1' appears in the column for its (conjoined) premise a '1' also appears in the same row in
the column for its conclusion; for an argument is
valid only if its conclusion is guaranteed to be true
if its premises are true. But then the proposition
that these premises (P) imply the conclusion (C), 'if
P then C', must be a tautology. The only possible
way for this proposition to be false is for its antecedent to be true while its consequent is false; and
the validity of the argument rules out this possibility.

EXERCISES

1. Use a truth-table to prove that the negation of a
   disjunction is equivalent to the conjunction of
   the negations of the antecedent and consequent
   of the disjunction.

2. Write down each of the traditional argument-forms
   discussed in section 2 above: (a) with infix notation, (b) with prefix notation, and (c) in the
   form of an implication (in both notations).

5. Special Properties of Implication

De Morgan's Theorem shows that we can always find an equivalent affirmative disjunction for every negative conjunction and an equivalent affirmative conjunction for every negative disjunction. The resulting equivalences appear below, using infix notation, where each form is equivalent to its counterpart in the other column:

N(p K q)	(Np A Nq)
N(Np K q)	(p A Nq)
N(p K Nq)	(Np A q)
N(Np K Nq)	(p A q)
N(p A q)	(Np K Nq)
N(Np A q)	(p K Nq)
N(p A Nq)	(Np K q)
N(Np A Nq)	(p K q)

The question naturally arises as to whether implications equivalent to these forms can also be found. The answer is obvious from the truth-table for implication, for we see there that an implication is false if and only if its antecedent is true while its consequent is false. Hence

'N(p C q)' is equivalent to '(p K Nq)',

and consequently

'p C q' is equivalent to 'N(p K Nq)'.

This information shows that we can extend De Morgan's Theorem, in effect, to include implication by adding a third column to the two given above:

(p C Nq)

(Np C Nq)

(p C q)

(Np C q)

N(Np C q)

N(p C q)

N(Np C Nq)

N(p C Nq)

where each form is equivalent to the corresponding
forms in the other two columns.

A little further consideration of the properties
of implication leads us to discover three tautologies
which are so surprising, or even counter-intuitive,
that they are called "the paradoxes of implication".
These tautologies are:

1. q C (p C q)

2. Np C (p C q)

3. (p K Np) C q

The first two can be seen easily in the truth-table
for implication, where it is clear that 'p C q' will
always be true when 'q' is true, or when 'p' is false:
the third follows from the fact that its antecedent,
'(p K Np)', must always be false because it is contradictory.

But the first tautology seems to say that a true
proposition is implied by anything whatever. If it
is true that there are monkeys in Brazil, then the
proposition that three is greater than two implies
that there are monkeys in Brazil; so does the proposition that snow is white, or that Baltimore is the
capital of the United States, or that all square
circles are pink, or anything else you care to imagine. Yet most of these "implications" do not
represent any logical connection at all. The second
tautology says that a false proposition implies
anything. Thus the proposition that some snakes are
mammals implies that the price of eggs is 90 cents a
dozen, that Mount Everest is in Russia, that equi-
lateral triangles have equal angles, and so forth.
The third tautology says that a contradiction implies
anything; this is really only a special case of what
the second tautology says.

Most of the "paradox" in these tautologies disappears
if we distinguish the rather vague general idea of
implication from the more specific idea of <u>logical</u>
implication or entailment. In the more general sense,

which is all that is required for the 'if...then---'
premises in the classical forms of argument, implication is a truth-function like conjunction and disjunction. Its truth or untruth depends only on the
truth-values of its components, regardless of their
content. From this standpoint, its properties are
no more paradoxical than those of the other truth-
functions. No one seems to find it "paradoxical",
for example, that from the fact that asparagus is
green we can infer that either asparagus is green or
God exists. In ordinary conversation, we use this
truth-functional kind of implication, "material
implication" as it is called, when we say things
like, "If he wins, I'll be a monkey's uncle," where
there is obviously no pretense of a logical connection between antecedent and consequent.

Logical implication, on the other hand, depends
on the specific content or forms of the propositions
involved, not just their truth-values. Thus it is
not a simple truth-functional relation. For example,
the propositions that Washington is the capital of
the U. S. and that the Library of Congress is in
Washington, taken together, logically imply that the
Library of Congress is in the capital of the U. S.
Here the truth of the antecedent conjunction guarantees the truth of the conclusion, by virtue of the
specific forms of the propositions. The fact that
this is so cannot be determined simply by examining
their truth-values. On the other hand, logical
implication and material implication are not toally
unrelated. If p logically implies q, then also p
materially implies q; for if p logically implies q
then it is impossible for q to be false when p is
true, so that it is impossible for 'if p then q' to
be false. We can account for this connection between
the two kinds of implication very simply, by suppos-
ing that a true logical implication is a necessarily
true implication, while a true material implication
(which is not also a logical one) is a contingently
true implication.

Now if we think in terms of logical rather than
material implication, the first two "paradoxes" of
implication disappear. For we cannot establish that
p logically implies q merely because q happens to be
true or because p happens to be false. The third
"paradox" does not disappear, for it is still tauto-
logically true that a contradiction implies anything.
But this is not particularly frightening. There is
no chance that the antecedent of this tautology will

ever be realized; the irresistible force will never meet the immovable object. If it did, then of course anything might happen.

The peculiar properties of implication make possible a fairly drastic simplication of the problem of evaluating certain kinds of complex arguments. We know that any truth-functional argument can be represented in the form of an implication-statement and that this implication must be a tautology if the argument is valid. Thus we can test the validity of the argument by determining whether the corresponding implication is indeed a tautology. This suggests that we should construct a truth-table for it. But in fact we do not need to construct the whole table. For we know that the implication is true <u>unless</u> its antecedent is true while its consequent is false. Hence we need only consider the possibility that the implication is false and determine whether this possibility can be consistently maintained. If it cannot, then the implication is a tautology and the argument valid; if it can, then the implication is not a tautology and the argument is not valid. Let us look at a concrete example.

Given the argument

> If either Israel withdraws from Sinai or oil is discovered in the Negev, there will be peace.

> Hence, if Israel withdraws from Sinai there will be peace

we see that this argument has the form

> If either p or q, then r

> Hence, if p then r

or, with infix notation,

$$(p \wedge q) \supset r$$

$$(p \supset r)$$

which can be expressed in the form of an implication as

$$((p \wedge q) \supset r) \supset (p \supset r)$$

In the more compact prefix notation, the argument is

CApqr
―――

Cpr

with the implication form

CCApqrCpr.

In order to decide whether or not this is a tautology,
without going through the cumbersome process of constructing a complete truth-table for it (which would
have eight rows and four columns in addition to the
three columns for the variables 'p', 'q' and 'r'), we
simply begin by assuming that the whole expression is
false; then we see what follows from this assumption.
First, if the implication as a whole is false, then
clearly its antecedent ('CApqr') is true and its consequent ('Cpr') is false. So we have

CCApqrCpr	CApqr	Cpr
0	1	0

Now the fact that 'CApqr' is true does not help us
much, because this can happen in three different ways,
as the table for implication shows. But the fact that
'Cpr' is false does help, because it shows that 'p'
must be true and 'r' must be false:

CCApqrCpr	CApqr	Cpr	p	r	Apq
1	1	0	1	0	1

And now it is clear that the value we assigned to
'CApqr' must be wrong, because that proposition must
be false if its antecedent ('Apq') is true while its
consequent ('r') is false. Thus we would have

CCApqrCpr	CApqr	Cpr	p	r	Apq
0	0	0	1	0	1

But now, finally, we see that the implication as a
whole cannot be false, as we originally assumed, because its antecedent turns out to be false after all;
if our assumption were correct, the antecedent would
have to be true. Hence our assumption was not correct,
and the implication must be a tautology.

A still more compact way of carrying out this
test for implications is to write down the values
immediately below the appropriate letters in the
expression. Suppose we have to evaluate the implication

$$((p \text{ C } q) \text{ C } r) \text{ C } ((p \text{ C } q) \text{ C } (p \text{ C } r)).$$

Assuming that the expression as a whole is false, we
write

$$((p \text{ C } q) \text{ C } r) \underset{0}{\text{C}} ((p \text{ C } q) \text{ C } (p \text{ C } r)),$$

letting the value placed under the main connective
'C' represent the value assumed for the whole proposition. Then since the antecedent '(p C q) c r' must be
true and the consequent '(p C q) C (p C r)' false, we
write

$$((p \text{ C } q) \underset{1}{\text{C}} r) \underset{0}{\text{C}} ((p \text{ C } q) \text{ C } \underset{0}{(p \text{ C } r)}).$$

Since we have a zero under the implication on the
right side, we must also put a '1' under its antecedent 'p C q' and a '0' under its consequent 'p C r':

$$((p \text{ C } q) \underset{1}{\text{C}} r) \underset{0}{\text{C}} ((p \underset{1}{\text{C}} q) \underset{0}{\text{C}} (p \underset{0}{\text{C}} r)).$$

Again, since 'p C r' is false, we know that 'p' must
be true and 'r' false:

$$((p \text{ C } q) \underset{1}{\text{C}} r) \underset{0}{\text{C}} ((p \underset{1}{\text{C}} q) \underset{0}{\text{C}} (\underset{1}{p} \underset{0}{\text{C}} \underset{0}{r})).$$

Now that we know the values of 'p' and 'r', we can
write them down under those leters wherever they occur:

$$((\underset{1}{p} \text{ C } q) \underset{1}{\text{C}} \underset{0}{r}) \underset{0}{\text{C}} ((\underset{1}{p} \underset{1}{\text{C}} q) \underset{0}{\text{C}} (\underset{1}{p} \underset{0}{\text{C}} \underset{0}{r})).$$

We see now that 'q' must be true, since it is the consequent of a true implication 'p C q' which has a true
antecedent 'p'. Also, that implication must be true in
both of its occurrences, so that we have

$$((\underset{1}{p} \underset{1}{\text{C}} \underset{1}{q}) \underset{1}{\text{C}} \underset{0}{r}) \underset{0}{\text{C}} ((\underset{1}{p} \underset{1}{\text{C}} \underset{1}{q}) \underset{0}{\text{C}} (\underset{1}{p} \underset{0}{\text{C}} \underset{0}{r})).$$

This result is inconsistent, because the antecedent
'(p C q) C r' cannot be true if it has a true antecedent 'p C q' and a false consequent 'r'. So we must
substitute a '0' for the '1' under the connective (C)
for the main antecedent:

$$((p \ C \ q) \ C \ r) \ C \ ((p \ C \ q) \ C \ (p \ C \ r))$$
$$\ \ \ 1 \ \ 1 \ \ 1 \ \ 1 \ 0 \ \ 0 \ \ \ \ 1 \ 1 \ 1 \ \ \ 0 \ \ 1 \ 00$$
$$\ \ \ \ \ \ \ \ \ \ \ \ \ 0$$

But now it is clear that the whole implication cannot
be false, as we had assumed, and it must be a tautology.

If an implication is not a tautology, on the other
hand, it will always be possible to find some assignment of values to its components which is consistent
with the assumption that it is false. For instance,
the implication

$$((p \ C \ q) \ K \ Np) \ C \ Nq,$$

which represents the fallacious argument known as
"denying the antecedent", can be evaluated as follows:

$$((p \ C \ q) \ K \ Np) \ C \ Nq$$
$$\ \ 0 \ 1 \ 1 \ \ 1 \ 10 \ \ 0 \ 01$$

showing that where 'p' is false and 'q' is true (as
in the third row of a complete truth-table) the implication as a whole is false. Note that the value for
the negation of a proposition is put down under the
'N'.

This short cut method for evaluating implications
naturally works best when the consequent of the implication is itself in the form of an implication or a
disjunction, or when the antecedent is in the form of
a conjunction. Otherwise, it may be necessary to consider two or three different assignments of values.
Consider

$$(p \ A \ (q \ K \ r)) \ C \ ((p \ A \ q) \ K \ (p \ A \ r))$$

for example. Here the information that the consequent
is false, or that the antecedent is true, is consistent
with three different possibilities in each case. But
the short-cut method can still be adapted to this situation; we simply carry it out three times, one for each
of the alternative possibilities. Thus we might have

```
(p A (q K r)) C ((p A q) K (p A r))
    1          0    1    0    0
    1          0    0    0    1
    1          0    0    0    0
```

in view of the three possible ways for the consequent
(K) to be false. In the first row it is obvious that
'p' and 'r' must both be false, on account of the zero
under 'p A r'. But then 'q K r' must also be false,
so that the antecedent 'p A (q K r)' cannot be true.
Thus the assignment of values in the first row is inconsistent. This does not establish that the whole
expression is a tautology, because the other two rows
must also be considered. A similar argument, however,
works for the remaining rows; and thus every possibility that the implication might be false is eliminated.

    Of course, the short-cut method works just as well
with prefix notation, and instead of

```
((p C q) K Nq) C Np
  1 1 0  1 10  0 01
    0      0
```

showing the validity of the classical argument by modus
tollens, we can write

```
CKCpqNqNp.
011101001
 00
```


                        EXERCISES

Evaluate by the short-cut method:

    1.   ((p C q) K (p C Nq)) C Np

    2.   (p K q) C N(Np A Nq)

    3.   (p C (q C r)) C (p C (r C q))

    4.   ((p C q) K (r C q)) C ((p A r) C q)

    5.   ((p K r) C q) C ((p C q) K (r C q))

VII.   LIMITATIONS OF TRADITIONAL LOGIC

1.   The Existential Import of Universals

We have seen that for every class of things, e.g.,

persons,

there is a corresponding complementary class,

non-persons,

which is the class of all those things that are not
persons.   This is guaranteed in traditional logic by
the obversion rule, according to which we can always
go from

Socrates is a person

to

Socrates is not a non-person

and vice versa, or from

Socrates is not a person

to

Socrates is a non-person

and vice versa.   We also saw earlier (chapter IV) how
the obversion of quantified propositions can be justified on the basis of the obversion of singulars.

Now the notion of a complementary class is formed
by a kind of limitation of, or subtraction from, the
class of all things, which is a universal class.   If
there is a class of non-persons, i.e., a class of all
things other than persons, then there must be a class
of all things, a universal class to which all things
belong, which may be exhaustively divided into "persons" and "non-persons".   (In principle, we should
consider the possibility that there may be things which
somehow fail to belong to either class; but since this
will make no essential difference to the main argument,
we ignore it here.)   Let us call this universal class
the class of

beings.

Clearly, it must be true that

All persons are beings

because the universal class, by definition, is all-inclusive; whatever is a member of any class must also be a member of the universal class. Hence, for the same reason, it must be true that

All non-persons are beings.

But now if we put these two results together and use the rules of traditional logic, we get a contradiction. Thus:

1.	All persons are beings	hypothesis
2.	All non-persons are beings	hypothesis
3.	All non-beings are persons	2, contra-position
4.	Some persons are non-beings	3, conversion by limitation
5.	Some persons are not beings	4, obversion

Step 5 is contradictory (by the square of opposition) to step 1. Since we have no reason to doubt that the first two propositions are true, there must be something wrong with the reasoning leading to the final step. But the only rules involved essentially are the rules for obversion, conversion and subalternation. This can be seen more clearly if we state the argument in a more expanded form:

1.	All persons are beings	hypothesis
2.	All non-persons are beings	hypothesis
3.	No non-persons are non-beings	2, obversion
4.	No non-beings are non-persons	3, conversion
5.	All non-beings are persons	4, obversion
6.	Some non-beings are persons	5, subalternation
7.	Some persons are non-beings	6, conversion
8.	Some persons are not beings	7, obversion

At step 3, the puzzling notion of "non-beings" appears; and in a sense it is obvious that this notion plays an essential role in the paradox. The class of non-beings must be an empty class if its complement ("beings") is universal. But there seems to be no way to prevent its appearance if the obversion rule is valid; and dropping the obversion rule would wreak so much havoc in logical theory that almost any alternative would be preferable. We should be able to infer, for example, that

it is false that some persons are non-beings

from the fact that

it is false that some persons are not beings,

since these two propositions are logically equivalent in virtue of the definition of complementary classes. For similar reasons, it does not seem plausible to raise any question about the rule of conversion (steps 4 and 7). Thus the rule of subalternation (step 6) stands out as the most questionable factor in the argument. If there are no "non-beings" at all, it is clearly impossible for some of them to be persons. But according to the traditional interpretation of universal propositions, step 5 should not be true either, for the same reason, although that step follows by simple obversion and conversion from what is given. Hence we should suspect that something is wrong with the traditional interpretation of universals.

This suspicion is confirmed when we examine what happens to propositions about empty classes in the square of opposition. Since anyone can make a mistake, for example, it seems altogether reasonable to believe that there are no infallible people. But if there are no infallible people, the class of infallible people must be an empty class. In that case, it should be false that

Some infallible people are geniuses

and equally false that

Some infallible people are not geniuses.

Yet according to the square of opposition, at least one of those propositions must be true. Otherwise, if they were both false, their contradictories

All infallible people are geniuses

and

No infallible people are geniuses

would both be true; and then, by the subalternation
rule, both of the particular propositions would be true
after all. Thus they would be both true and false,
which is absurd. It appears, therefore, that according
to traditional logic we must believe in the existence
of infallible people, to avoid absurdity. The same
goes for unicorns, leprechauns, flying saucers, rectan-
gular circles, and so forth.

To find the source of the difficulty, we must remind ourselves that we have been assuming that the four
types of quantified (A, E, I, O) propositions are de-
finable in terms of sets of singulars of the form

s_1 is a P

s_2 is a P

s_3 is a P

. . . . .

s_n is a P

for any pair of subject and predicate terms (S, P). We
have assumed that the A-proposition ('All S are P')
signifies that each of these singulars is true; the I-
proposition, that at least one of them is true; the E-
proposition, that each of them is false; and the O-
proposition, that at least one of them is false. Moreover, we have assumed that when a singular, like

s_1 is a P,

is false, then the corresponding negative form

s_1 is not a P

is true. But suppose that the class "S" has no members
at all. How can this sort of interpretation work? If
there are no leprechauns at all, there is no such thing
as a "first leprechaun", a "second leprechaun", and so
on. And then it is clearly false that (or not true
that) the first leprechaun is a pixie; yet it cannot
be true that the first leprechaun is not a pixie either.

Both the affirmative and the negative singular would
have to be rejected. This suggests that the notion of
the singular proposition needs further examination, and
we shall come to that later on. But for the present
let us continue to work with the traditional notion.
Our problem then is to see whether we can find some new
way of interpreting quantified propositions, in terms
of singulars, so as to avoid the paradoxes we have
discussed.

The problem with our old method was that we allowed
ourselves, implicitly, to formulate singulars referring
to non-existent individuals (like "the first non-being"
or "the tenth infallible person") because we had to deal
with quantified propositions mentioning classes of such
individuals. How can we interpret propositions of this
type without permitting the unwanted inference that non-
existent individuals exist?

One way to do this is to formulate our singulars
in terms of individuals whose existence or reality is
above suspicion, being the members of a class that has
members beyond any possible doubt. Is there such a
class? Yes, there is the class of all beings, the
universal class. If any class has members, the universal class must have them. Let us refer to these
members as

$$u_1, u_2, u_3, \ldots, u_n, \ldots$$

which we presume to be infinitely numerous. For any
given predicate term, 'P', we can now formulate the
usual affirmative set of singular propositions

u_1 is a P, etc.

and the usual negative set

u_1 is not a P, etc.

But since the predicate term may designate an empty
class, we do not assume that there are such individuals
as

$p_1, \quad p_2, \quad p_3, \quad$ etc.

unless we happen to know that some members of the
universal class are members of P.

The idea expressed in the I-proposition ('Some S
are P') is that some members of S are also member of P;

- 145 -

in other words, some members of the universal class that are members of S are also members of P. If this is the case, there must be some individual (u_n) such that

u_n is an S and u_n is a P.

Since this is a conjunction of two singulars with the same subject term, we can now interpret the I-proposition in terms of the set of all such conjunctions:

u_1 is an S and u_1 is a P

u_2 is an S and u_2 is a P

u_3 is an S and u_3 is a P

. . . .

u_n is an S and u_n is a P

. . . .

The I-proposition is true if and only if at least one of these conjunctions is true.

The idea expressed in the O-proposition ('Some are not P') is that some members of S are not also members of P, so that at least one member of the universal class is a member of S without being a member of P:

u_n is an S and u_n is not a P.

Hence we can formulate the set

u_1 is an S and u_1 is not a P

u_2 is an S and u_2 is not a P

u_3 is an S and u_2 is not a P

. . . .

u_n is an S and u_n is not a P

. . . .

so that the O-proposition is true if and only if at least one of these conjunctions is true.

Let us now refer to the first set of conjunctions as "the I-set" and the second set of conjunctions as "the O-set".

Since each of the universal (A, E) propositions
is contradictory to one of the particulars (O, I), we
should be able to interpret them in terms of the same
sets. Thus the A-proposition ('All S are P') is true
if and only if each conjunction in the O-set is <u>false</u>.
But if

> It is false that both u_n is an S and u_n is
> not a P

then by De Morgan's Theorem (chapter 6)

> Either u_n is not an S or u_n is a P,

or equivalently

> If u_n is an S then u_n is a P.

Thus we have three formally different but equivalent
interpretations for the A-proposition: (1) as the
set of the negations of the members of the O-set, (2)
as the equivalent set of disjunctions, or (3) as the
equivalent set of implications. In practice, it is
usually most convenient to make use of the third.

Similarly, since the E-proposition ('No S are P')
is contradictory to the I-proposition, it is true if
and only if each member of the I-set is false. But if

> It is false that u_n is an S and u_n is a P

then by De Morgan's Theorem

> Either u_n is not an S or u_n is not a P,

or equivalently

> If u_n is an S then u_n is not a P.

Thus we also have three different but equivalent interpretations for the E-proposition.

The essential difference between these new interpretations and the older ones is that the new ones do
not ascribe <u>existential import</u> to universal propositions.
That is, we no longer assume that the classes mentioned
in true universal propositions have members, although
we still assume that the classes mentioned in true particular propositions do. But the assumption that universals have existential import was the basis of the
traditional subalternation rule; without it, the rule

fails. The advantage is that we can no longer derive
the paradoxical results associated with the presence
of empty classes, and we can preserve the consistency
of our logic. The disadvantage is, of course, that
our logic is somewhat weaker than before, as will be
seen in the next section.

EXERCISES

Using the new interpretations of quantified propositions and the rules for truth functions (chapter 6),
show why

1. The I-proposition is equivalent to its
   converse

2. The E-proposition is equivalent to its
   converse

   (Hint: use the disjunctive interpretation
           for the E)

3. The A-proposition is equivalent to its
   converse

4. The O-proposition is equivalent to its
   contrapositive

2. Logic Without Subalternation

It is obvious that when we drop the traditional
subalternation rule we can no longer rely on those
forms of inference which were derived with the help
of that rule. This fact is most striking in connection with the square of opposition, although it also
affects conversion, contraposition and the categorical
syllogism.

In the square of opposition, the contradiction
rule remains intact; but without the subalternation
rule we cannot show that the universals are contrary
to each other. When "S" is an empty class, 'All S
are P' and 'No S are P' are both true, because their
contradictories ('Some S are not P' and 'Some S are
P') are both false. Thus, if there are no unicorns,

It is false that some unicorns are mammals

and

It is false that some unicorns are not mammals.

Therefore, by the contradiction rule,

All unicorns are mammals

and

No unicorns are mammals.

This result is odd but quite harmless if we interpret universals in the new way. For by 'All unicorns are mammals' we need only mean that

If anything is a unicorn, then it is a mammal;

and this is obviously true if there are no unicorns at all. If there are no unicorns, then for any given member (u_n) of the universal class it is false that u_n is a unicorn, so that by the truth-table for implication

If u_n is a unicorn, then u_n is a mammal

must be true for every member of the universal class. Similarly, by 'No unicorns are mammals' we need only mean that

If anything is a unicorn, then it is not a mammal,

which must also be true for the same reasons.

The traditional rule that I and O are sub-contraries, so that if one of them is false the other is true, also fails in the absence of subalternation because, as we have seen, both of the particular propositions are false when their subject-term designates an empty class. To show that O is true if I is false, for example, we have to argue that E is true if I is false (by the contradiction rule) and that O follows from E. But of course the latter step depends on subalternation.

Clearly the superalternation rule also fails; we cannot now show that the universals are false if their subalternates are false, since the proof depends on the validity of subalternation.

Thus the only inferences that remain valid in the square of opposition are those representing the contradiction rule: The A and O propositions still must have opposite truth-values, and so must the E and I propositions. In place of the traditional subalternation rule however, we can now use what I shall call a rule of conditional subalternation:

> If there is at least one S, then 'Some are P' may be inferred from 'All S are P', and 'Some S are not P' may be inferred from 'No S are P'.

This rule can easily be justified in terms of the new interpretations for quantified propositions. Then we can also show corresponding conditional rules for contraries, sub-contraries and superalternates. That is,

> If there is at least one S, then the universals are contraries, the particulars are subcontraries, and the universals are superalternates of the subalternates.

The reader should be able to see how this rule can be derived from the rule of conditional subalternation.

Obviously the traditional rules for conversion and contraposition "by limitation" also fail in the absence of subalternation. Since the converse by limitation of an A-proposition is really the converse of its subalternate, we cannot validly infer it from the A-proposition unless we have the subalternation rule. On the other hand, we can still have a conditional rule permitting conversion by limitation, based on the rule of conditional subalternation. Similar remarks apply to contraposition by limitation. Therefore:

> If there is at least one S, then conversion by limitation and contraposition by limitation may be used.

The categorical syllogism is also affected. This is most obvious in the case of the "weakened" syllogisms, where a particular conclusion is drawn from premises that would justify a universal conclusion. For example, in

All M are P

All S are M

Hence, some S are P

there is a tacit use of the subalternation rule, which

appears in both of the two possible derivations of this argument (from the AAA or the AII moods in the first figure). More generally, we can see that any categorical syllogism drawing a particular (I,O) conclusion from universal premises must involve the assumption that the class denoted by the minor term ('S') is non-empty; and our new interpretation of universal propositions does not justify this assumption. Thus all of these traditionally recognized forms of the categorical syllogism which depend on it must now be rejected, namely (listing them by figure):

I: AAI, EAO

II: AEO, EAO

III: AAI, EAO

IV: AAI, AEO, EAO.

A rule which is necessary and sufficient to eliminate just these forms from our list of valid syllogisms is the following:

> No particular conclusion may be drawn from universal premises,

which may be called the <u>existential rule</u>. By means of it we can eliminate such an argument as

> All square circles are squares
>
> All square circles are circles
>
> Hence, some circles are squares,

which is obviously invalid because it draws a false conclusion from true premises, but which does not violate any of the traditional rules.

It was said earlier (V.2) that in the modern theory of the syllogism we do not need to assume the third quality-rule, the rule that is no premise is negative the conclusion must be affirmative. This is because every syllogistic form that would be eliminated by the traditional set of rules would also be eliminated by the same set with the new existential rule replacing the third quality-rule. We can show this by considering all possible cases of syllogistic moods with two affirmative premises and a negative conclusion. Disregarding the order of the premises, there are six cases to consider: AAE, AAO, AIE, AIO, IIE, IIO. Details are left to the reader as an exercise.

It also happens that in the presence of the new existential rule the distribution theorem (Theorem I, in V.3) takes a stronger form. For now we can show that the number of distributed terms (D-terms) in the premises must be <u>exactly</u> one more than the number of D-terms in the conclusion. This is done by showing that there is <u>at most</u> one more D-term in the premises: we consider the possible cases in which they have two, three or four more D-terms, showing that no valid syllogism is obtained in any of these cases. This proof is also left to the reader.

The modern interpretation of universals, now generally known as the "Boolean interpretation" in honor of the English mathematician and logician George Boole (1815-64) weakens the traditional assumption that the fundamental form of categorical proposition is the singular form. According to the Boolean interpretation, universal propositions may be true even though none of the corresponding singulars is true. On the other hand, the traditional view remains intact in the sense that singular propositions are still the basic units or "atoms" in our analysis up to this point. But there are some problems about singulars, as we shall see shortly, which suggest that in the long run we may not be able to sustain this analysis.

EXERCISES

1. Show how the rule of conditional subalternation can be justified in terms of the Boolean interpretation of universals.

2. Derive similar conditional rules for contraries, sub-contraries and superalternates.

3. Show that the number of distributed terms in a categorical syllogism must be <u>at most</u> one greater than the number of distributed terms in the conclusion, if we assume that no valid syllogisms can draw a particular conclusion from two universal premises.

4. Show why the third "quality rule" for the syllogism (that if no premise is negative the conclusion must be affirmative) is not needed if we assume that no

valid syllogism can draw a particular conclusion
from two universal premises.

3. Singular Propositions Revisited

Although for most purposes we have treated singulars as being the basic unanalyzed units of logical
discourse, we did suggest (in chapter 2) that they can
be understood as assertions about sets of identity-
statements. This gave us a ready explanation for the
traditional concept of "distribution of terms", which
figures so prominently in the traditional formulation
of logical rules. The basis for this interpretation
was our assumption that we can always treat the predicate term of a singular as the name of some class
(or extensional attribute), so that the proposition
asserts or denies that some individual is identical
with one of the members of this class. But we did
not examine the concept of identity itself.

Every individual (and indeed every thing or being)
is the same as itself and different from every other
individual; it is exactly what it is. For every member
(u) of the universal class, we can always assert that

u is identical with u

or, using the equality-sign for identity,

u = u

Moreover, we can assert that

Necessarily u = u.

For it it were not necessary that an individual is the
same as itself, it would be possible that it is different from itself; and this "possibility" does not seem
to be coherent or conceivable at all.

It frequently happens that there are two or more
names for the same individual in ordinary language. For
instance, Aristotle and "the Stagirite" are the same
person. Since this is the case, everything that is
true about Aristotle is also true about the Stagirite,
and vice versa. In other words, we can substitute the
one name for the other in any proposition where one of
them occurs. But notice that the names themselves
('Aristotle', 'the Stagirite') are different, not
identical, and not everything that is true about one
name is also true about the other. Thus Plato did not

know that Aristotle, his pupil would later be given
the name 'the Stagirite'. Presumably he knew that

        Aristotle = the Stagirite

because this proposition means the same as that

        Aristotle = Aristotle.

More generally, suppose that 'x' and 'y' are different names for the same individual, so that

        x = y

is true, and suppose that '(...x...)' is some proposition mentioning x, and that '(...y...)' is the result
of substituting 'y' for 'x' in the same proposition.
Then if

        (...x...)

is true, so is

        (...y...).

In other words, when two expressions are names of the
same thing, they may be substituted for each other in
any context. This is sometimes referred to as
"Leibniz' law" for identity.

        It is important to remember that the name of an
individual, e.g.,

        Aristotle,

is not the same as the name of that name, e.g.,

        'Aristotle'.

Thus Leibniz' law does not permit us to go from

        'The Stagirite' is a definite description

to

        'Aristotle' is a definite description.

        In view of Leibniz' law, it is tempting to suppose
that an identity statement of the form ' x = y' is just
a way of saying that the two expressions 'x' and 'y'
have exactly the same meaning. If this were so, it

would explain why they can always be substituted for
each other. It would also account for the fact that
'x = y' may be interesting, informative and (apparently) contingent, while 'x = x' and 'y = y' are uninteresting and uninformative though logically necessary.

But the trouble is that the meanings of expressions
are fixed by the historical evolution of language, by
convention, or by arbitrary stipulation; and clearly
the truth of such a statement as, say,

Oxford is the oldest English university

depends on something more than linguistic convention
or stipulation. Hence it seems more plausible to
think of identity-statements as statements about the
individuals or things named rather than about the
names or expressions themselves. But then how do we
account for the apparent difference in meaning between
the forms 'x = y' and ' x = x'?

One proposed solution, which has gained fairly
wide approval, is that of the German philosopher,
logician and mathematician Gottlob Frege (1848-1925).
Frege argued that we should distinguish between two
sorts of meaning: the "sense" of an expression and
the "denotation" (or "reference") of an expression.
This was essentially the traditional distinction between the "intensional" and "extensional" meanings
of terms, except that the traditional distinction
applied to common names (of attributes) only, while
Frege's was supposed to apply to proper names and
even to sentences. In an identity of the form 'x =
y', he suggested, the terms 'x' and 'y' may have
different senses although they denote (or refer to)
the same individual. Now since the same distinction
of sense and denotation applies to sentences as well
as terms, we can also say that a sentence of the form
'x = y' or 'x = x' has both a sense and a denotation.
It seems natural to assume further that sentences of
these forms must have different senses if the terms
'x' and 'y' themselves have different senses. This
accounts for the apparent divergence in meaning of
the sentences. And Frege supposed that these sentences could be said to have the same denotation if
they have the same truth-value and different denotations if they have different truth-values; they would
be said to denote "the True" or "the False".

Although many people find this approach persuasive and elegant, it is not without difficulties. For

one thing, it is not clear that proper names, common names and sentences can all have "senses" and "denotations" in the same way. If they do, and if 'x = y' is true whenever 'x' and 'y' have the same denotation, then we should be able to substitute complete sentences for 'x' and 'y' in the formula 'x = y'. But if we do so we get nonsense. It is clear enough that we can say something like

Cicero is the same as Tully

or like

Cicero is the same as Cicero;

but what could be meant by saying something like

Cicero is the same as Tully is the same as
Cicero is the same as Tully

or something like

Cicero is the same as Tully is the same as
Cicero is the same as Cicero?

The latter sayings do not even qualify as sentences. Of course, we can say something like

'Cicero is the same as Tully' is the same
as 'Cicero is the same as Tully'

or, speaking falsely,

'Cicero is the same as Tully' is the same as
'Cicero is the same as Cicero',

which are perfectly good sentences. But here we are using the names of the sentences 'Cicero is the same as Tully' and 'Cicero is the same as Cicero', not those sentences themselves; and we are asserting (according to Frege's theory) that these names have the same denotation, i.e., that they are names of the same sentence. We have not asserted that the sentences themselves have the same denotation, i.e., that they are both true or both false. The problem is, then, how can we arrive at this kind of assertion? We might come fairly close to it by saying something like

That Cicero is the same as Tully is the same
as that Cicero is the same as Cicero,

which is grammatically sound. But the terms in this

identity-statement ('that Cicero is the same as Tully' and 'that Cicero is the same as Cicero') are obviously not sentences but rather substantive phrases. These phrases must have some denotation; but what? If they denote sentences, names of sentences, or senses of sentences, then the statement as a whole will turn out to be false, and we have not arrived at the assertion we wanted to make. If they could denote the denotations of sentences (i.e., "the True" or "the False") they would be sentences themselves, which they are not.

Frege's method of dealing with identity is not the only method available. Another method is to treat proper names as having denotations only (not sense) and sentences as having senses but not denotations, which is more in accord with traditional theories of meaning. The peculiar features of identity-statements which Frege's theory was designed to explain can then be handled by assuming that in most every-day situations these statements are really abbreviations or ellipses for more complicated quantified propositions. Some details of this will be examined shortly. The alternative method also has the advantage that it can take account of the following curious result of our basic rules for identity.

The curious result is this: if any identity is true, then it is necessarily true. For if we suppose that

$$x = y,$$

then since we know that

$$\text{Necessarily } x = x$$

it follows by Leibniz' law that

$$\text{Necessarily } x = y,$$

substituting 'y' for the right-hand occurrence of 'x'. Thus if it is true that Aristotle is identical to the Stagirite, then

$$\text{Necessarily Aristotle} = \text{the Stagirite.}$$

This result raises a difficulty for our interpretation of singular propositions. We assumed earlier that any affirmative singular,

$$x \text{ is a } P,$$

asserts in effect that one of the identities

$$x = p_1$$

$$x = p_2$$

etc.

is true. But now it appears that if any of these identities is true then it is necessarily true; and from this it is easy to show that it is necessarily true that one of the identities is true. Thus what the singular proposition asserts, according to our earlier interpretation, must be necessarily true, so that from 'x is a P' we could always infer that

Necessarily x is a P.

Hence also from 'x is not a P', by way of its observe ('x is a non-P'), we could infer that necessarily x is a non-P and therefore that

Necessarily x is not a P.

These results would be disastrous because they would erase the distinction between necessary and contingent truth or falsehood. Surely we do not want to be forced to the conclusion that

James Joyce necessarily wrote <u>Ulysses</u>

merely because, in fact,

James Joyce wrote <u>Ulysses</u>,

as if that fact were some sort of logical truth.

Apparently then, our interpretation of singulars in terms of identities will not do, and we cannot rely on it for an explanation of the traditional doctrine of distribution. But we shall come back to this question later. Meanwhile, there is still another problem to be faced.

We said earlier (chapter 2) that the subject term of a singular proposition must always be a proper name, i.e., the name of some individual, and must therefore be either a proper noun (like 'Jefferson') or a definite description (like 'the architect of Monticello'). By this test,

Jefferson designed Monticello

is a genuine singular proposition, assuming that there
is (or was) such an individual as Jefferson. And that

Jefferson did not design Monticello

is also a genuine singular, though false. But by the
same test we should rule out both

The Easter Bunny likes carrots

and

The Easter Bunny does not like carrots,

on the theory that there is no such individual as the
Easter Bunny.

Aristotle himself rejected this view. According
to him, sentences about non-existent individuals are
false rather than meaningless. Thus he would have said
that 'The Easter Bunny likes carrots' is a false
singular proposition. And he would have said that
'The Easter Bunny does not like carrots' is therefore
true, if we take it to mean that

It is false that the Easter Bunny is a
carrot-liker;

but it is not true that

The Easter Bunny is a non-carrot-liker.

These two sentences are equivalent according to the
traditional rule of obversion, but Aristotle never
accepted that rule and went out of his way to avoid
using it in his reduction-proofs for syllogisms.

In one sense, Aristotle's instincts in this
matter were better than those of his successors until
very recently; for we know now that it is quite possible and convenient to interpret propositions about
non-existent individuals in the way he suggests. But
the modern view depends on a new method of handling
singulars with descriptive phrases (like 'the Easter
Bunny') which was not available to him. If a proposition of the form

The so-and-so is a P

is false because there is no such thing as "the so-and-so", then its negation, with the same subject-term,

The so-and-so is not a P

should also be false for the same reason. Otherwise, we would have to assume that although the affirmative form mentions some supposed individual ("the so-and-so"), the negative form where the same phrase occurs, does not. The consequences of this assumption would be disastrous. Negative propositions would become (to use a modern phrase) referentially opaque: We would not be able to carry out substituions by Leibniz' law in such propositions. Thus although we could still go from (or to)

George Washington was a Texan

to (or from)

The first President of the U. S. was a Texan,

given that George Washington was the first President of the U. S., we could not go from (or to)

George Washington was not a Texan

to (or from)

The first President of the U. S. was not a Texan,

because, theoretically, Washington would be mentioned only in the affirmative singular, not in the negative one. This result could not be reconciled with the classical rules of inference or with the traditional interpretation of quantified propositions.

The more generally accepted view was that every singular term (noun or descriptive phrase) in a singular proposition must be regarded as a proper name. This view has the merit of avoiding the difficulty just mentioned, but it has difficulties of its own. For it implies that there are no propositions about non-existent individuals, just as (according to traditional theory) there are no propositions about empty classes.

Suppose it is argued, then, that no singular proposition can be formulated about "the Easter Bunny" because there is no such individual. The main premise in this argument is that

There is no such individual as the Easter Bunny,

and this must be construed as a genuine proposition of
some sort if it is to serve as premise for an argument.
If we construe it as a singular, i.e.,

The Easter Bunny is not an individual,

then clearly the argument fails, since this is a proposition of the very type supposed to be excluded by the
argument. If we construe it as a universal negative,
i.e.,

No individual is the Easter Bunny,

we are saying, for each member (u) of the universal
class, that

u is not the Easter Bunny.

But this is evidently the negation of an identity-
statement ('u is the Easter Bunny') and is logically
equivalent to

The Easter Bunny is not u,

which leaves us with the same problem as before. We
might try to escape this result by interpreting the
statement, 'There is no such individual as the Easter
Bunny', as a statement not about the Easter Bunny but
only about the name of the Easter Bunny, e.g.,

'The Easter Bunny' does not designate an
individual.

Then we could reformulate the conclusion as

'The Easter Bunny' is not the subject term
of any singular,

or something of that sort. The trouble with this approach
is that there is no good reason to grant the premise.
Why should I not let 'The Easter Bunny' designate some
individual, if I wish to? The only sound objection
would be that there is no such individual as the Easter
Bunny; and this objection brings us back to the starting
point.

Clearly there is no such individual as the Easter
Bunny if there is no such thing as an Easter Bunny, i.e.,
if the class of Easter Bunnies is empty. But there may

be no such individual even if the class is not empty, because there may be more than one. For example, there is no such individual as the author of <u>Mutiny on the Bounty</u>, because there are two authors (Nordoff and Hall). More generally, there is no such thing as

> the so-and-so

if and only if

> either there is no so-and-so, or there is more than one so-and-so.

Consequently, it must be true that

> there is such a thing as the so-and-so

if and only if

> there is at least one so-and-so, and there is at most one so-and-so.

These equivalences will give us a solution to the problem of how to deal with non-existent individuals and, in addition, a new interpretation for singular propositions. Let 'S' represent the "so-and-so" class. Then in order to say that there is no such individual as the S, we need only say that either there is no S or there is more than one S; and this statement makes no mention of "the S". The Easter Bunny is real if and only if there is exactly one Easter Bunny. We can make use of this idea in connection with any singular proposition of the form

> The S is a P.

This form can now be understood as a way of saying:

> There is exactly one S, and every S is a P.

Notice again that there is no mention of "the S" in this interpretation. The negative form,

> The S is not a P,

can be interpreted in two different ways:

(1)   It is false that (both)there is exactly one S and every S is a P,

or

(2)   There is exactly one S, and it is false that
         every S is a P.

On the second interpretation, but not the first, we can
justify obversion of the negative singular.

     The ideas involved in this way of interpreting
singular propositions were first developed by the late
Bertrand Russell, and today they are known as "Russell's
theory of descriptions". We shall explore some of their
implications for logic and philosophy in the next
section.

                    EXERCISES

Using the theory of descriptions just presented, show
how to justify the inference from 'The S is not a P' to
'The S is a non-P', given that there is exactly one S.

4.   Applications of the Theory of Descriptions

     The theory of descriptions can be readily extended
so as to cover singular propositions and identity-
statements of all types. This is because we can always
replace a proper noun (like 'Napoleon') by a definite
description (like 'the person generally known as
Napoleon'), although we cannot always replace a definite
description by a proper noun. A proper noun cannot
usually be relied upon to designate one and only one
individual. Thus 'Napoleon' may, for all we know,
designate not only the famous French general but also
various other persons, dogs, cats, other household pets,
and so forth. A definite description, on the other
hand, can be made as detailed as necessary to avoid
ambiguity. It is convenient to use proper nouns, of
course, as long as we are not worried about absolute
precision. But it is important to understand that we
do not have to use them, and we can always substitute
some descriptive phrase referring to the same individual.

     Thus whenever we use a proper noun ('N') as sub-
ject of a singular, such as

     N is a P,

we can always interpret that noun as an abbreviation for
some descriptive phrase ('the individual designated by
'N', or more simply 'the "N"'), so that the proposition

becomes

The "N" is a P,

which means, according to the theory of descriptions:

There is exactly one "N", and every "N" is a P.

The negative singular,

N is not a P,

may be interpreted as

The "N" is not a P,

which means either

(1)   It is false that there is exactly one "N" and
        every "N" is a P

or

(2)   There is exactly one "N", and it is false that
        every "N" is a P.

Notice that the first interpretation is weaker, and
thereby logically safer than the second. If the second
is true, then the first is also true, but not vice
versa. In most everyday situations, the second is
probably intended; but for purposes of logical analysis
we must be careful not to assume it without adequate
justification.

Since we can always substitute definite descriptions for proper nouns, we can do so in identity
statements as well as in singulars of the classical type.
So whenever we have

a = b,

where 'a' and 'b' are proper nouns, we can take it to
mean

The "a" = the "b".

This may be understood as an abbreviation for

There is exactly one "a", and there is
exactly one "b", and every "a" is identical
with every "b".

Recalling that "a" and "b" are the classes of individuals designated by 'a' and 'b' respectively, let 'x' and 'y' stand for any arbitrarily chosen individuals. Then to say that every "a" is identical with every "b" is to say that

> if x is an "a" and y is a "b", then x = y.

Similarly, when we have

> a = a,

this will mean that

> the "a" = the "a"

or

> there is exactly one "a", and every "a" is
> identical with every "a".

In other words,

> there is exactly one "a", and if x is an "a"
> then x = x.

We argued earlier that every individual is necessarily, not merely contingently, identical with itself. But now, in virtue of the theory of descriptions, we can see that the statement

> Necessarily a = a

is ambiguous in the same way as a negative singular is ambiguous. For we can take it to mean

> Necessarily the "a" = the "a",

and then we have to choose between

(1)   Necessarily there is exactly one "a" and every
           "a" is identical with every "a"

or

(2)   There is exactly one "a", and necessarily
           every "a" is identical with every "a".

The second interpretation is weaker and must be chosen except in those particular cases where we can prove that there is exactly one "a". Otherwise, from the true proposition

      Necessarily the Taj Mahal = the Taj Mahal

we could draw the false conclusion that

      Necessarily there is exactly one Taj Mahal.

But the existence of the Taj Mahal is obviously a matter of contingent fact rather than logical necessity. We see also that

      Necessarily a = b,

or

      Necessarily the "a" = the "b",

is ambiguous, since we must choose between

(1)   Necessarily there is exactly one "a" and there is exactly one "b" and every "a" is identical with every "b"

or

(2)   There is exactly one "a" and there is exactly one "b", and necessarily every "a" is identical with every "b".

Here again the second interpretation is the only safe one in most cases.

      Now we have a way of explaining those identity statements, frequently used in ordinary discourse, which are intended as statements of contingent fact rather than logical necessity. Consider for example the statement

      Shakespeare is the author of <u>Hamlet</u>.

This seems to mean that

      Shakespeare is identical with the author of <u>Hamlet</u>.

But if this is what it means, and if we take 'Shakespeare' and 'the author of <u>Hamlet</u>' simply as proper names, then they must either be names for the same individual or names for different individuals. If they are names for the same individual, then since every individual is necessarily identical with itself it will follow that

- 166 -

Shakespeare is necessarily the author of Hamlet. This is much stronger than what we intended to say. On the other hand, if 'Shakespeare' and 'the author of Hamlet' are names for different individuals, then it must be false that Shakespeare is the author of Hamlet, contrary to what we intended. Using the theory of descriptions, however, we can interpret the original statement as follows:

> There is exactly one "Shakespeare" and there is exactly one author of Hamlet, and every "Shakespeare" is identical with an author of Hamlet.

So interpreted, the statement as a whole is contingent. It is in the form of a conjunction, the antecedent of which is clearly contingent on the historical fact of there being just one Shakespeare and just one author of Hamlet. Hence although it is true that Shakespeare is the author of Hamlet, it is also true that

> Shakespeare is not necessarily the author of Hamlet,

because the truth in question is a contingent truth.

Let us return now to a question that was left hanging at the beginning of the last section: how shall we deal with the traditional concept of "distribution of terms" if we can no longer interpret singular propositions as originally suggested, by way of sets of identity-statements? The question was really premature, for if we make use of the theory of descriptions the problem that gave rise to it is no longer a problem. It was argued that we should not interpret

> x is a P

as a way of saying that one of the identities

> x = p_1
>
> x = p_2
>
> etc.

is true, since if any of them is true it is necessarily true, with the result that the original singular would also be necessarily true. This difficulty disappears when we note that 'p_1' is simply a shorthand for 'the first member of P', so that we can understand 'x = p_1' to mean

> There is exactly one first member of P, and
> x is identical with every first member of P.

So interpreted, the "identity" of x with p_1 is contingently true or false; and of course the same reasoning applies to the other members of P. Therefore the characteristics of identity do not, after all, pose any serious problem for the original interpretation of singular propositions suggested nor for the traditional concept of distribution.

EXERCISES

Find a correct (or preferable) interpretation, according to the theory of descriptions, for each of the following.

1. The largest island is Australia.

2. Nixon is an ex-President.

3. The Commander in Chief of the Armed Forces is not a military man.

4. Rumpelstiltskin is not a real person.

5. The first astronaut to land on Mars is not a Brazilian.

VIII. NEW DIRECTIONS

1. Many-valued Logics

We have seen that modern logical theory has parted company with traditional logic by recognizing the existence of empty classes and by developing a new interpretation for singular propositions. More recently it has become clear that we need not limit ourselves to the classical truth-values (true, false) and that we can formulate logical systems with three, four or indeed any number of values. Even traditional logic, one might argue, is really a four-valued system to the extent that it recognizes a distinction between necessary and contingent truth and falsehood. This four-valued system simply amounts to a scheme for splitting each of the more general truth-values into two parts, so that the traditional law of excluded middle (that every proposition is either true or false) still holds.

But we can also formulate systems with odd numbers of truth-values (3, 5, etc.) in which the law of excluded middle fails. At first sight, this looks impossible. For if we try to express the denial of the law of excluded middle, we find ourselves saying that for some proposition (p)

it is false that either p or not p,

or, with infix notation.

N(p A Np),

which has the form of a negative disjunction. According to De Morgan's Theorem, a negative disjunction is equivalent to the conjunction of the negations of its components. Hence, the negation of the law of excluded middle is equivalent to

Np K NNp

or

p K Np,

which is a simple contradiction. Hence we cannot consistently formulate a logical system in which the law of excluded middle is denied. Nevertheless, that law might fail in the sense that it is not _provable_ in the system, even though it is not denied. If we do not

assert the law of excluded middle, it does not follow
that we must deny it; to assume otherwise is really to
assume the law of excluded middle itself.

Let us see what happens, then, if we assume a
third truth-value intermediate between "truth" and
"falsehood". Let us say that a proposition having
this third value is indefinite. In order to investi-
gate this idea, we shall use a slight modification of
the truth-table method.

Under the truth-table method, we represent truth-
functional relationships by way of a column of values
for each expression, where each entry represents the
value of the expression given certain values for its
compoents. Thus for the basic truth-functions we have:

p	q	Np	Nq	Kpq	Apq	Cpq	Epq
1	1	0	0	1	1	1	1
1	0	0	1	0	1	0	0
0	1	1	0	0	1	1	0
0	0	1	1	0	0	1	1

Now instead of using a column we can use a matrix in
each case, as follows:

p	q		Np	Nq	Kpq	Apq	Cpq	Epq
1	1		1 0	0 0	0 1 1 0	1 1	1 0	1 0
0	0		1 0	1 1	0 1 0 0	1 0	1 1	0 1

The upper row of each matrix contains the first two
entries in the truth-table column, written from left to
right instead of vertically; the lower row contains the
remaining values. Thus the upper row represents the
values for any expression when its antecedent (p) is
true, and the lower row represents the values when the
antecedent is false. Similarly, the left column represents the values for the expression when its consequent (q) is true, and the right column represents the
values when the consequent is false. If the normal
antecedent and consequent are transposed, then the
upper right and lower left entries are correspondingly
transposed, so that for 'Cqp' we have

1 1
0 1,

although of course this transposition makes no difference in the matrices for conjunction, disjunction or
equivalence.

The matrix method works only for truth-functions
containing no more than two variables (p, q), but it
is very convenient for dealing with three or more truth-
values. Assuming now that we have three values (0, 1,
2) instead of the traditional two (0, 1), and that the
new value is intermediate between "true" and "false",
we shall let '0' stand for falsehood as before but now
'1' will stand for the new intermediate value and '2'
for truth. Hence the standard truth-table columns for
the variables would be

        p q
        ───
        2 2
        2 1
        2 0
        1 2
        1 1
        1 0
        0 2
        0 1
        0 0

with the corresponding matrices

        222   210
        111   and 210
        000   210.

Now the basic matrices for two-valued logic can be re-
written in terms of three-valued matrices, by substituting '2' for '1' and by placing the four numerals at the
corners of the new three-by-three matrix. Thus we have

p	q	Np	Nq	Kpq	Apq	Cpq	Epq
2-2	2-0	0-0	0-2	2-0	2-2	2-0	2-0
---	---	---	---	---	---	---	---
0-0	2-0	2-2	0-2	0-0	2-0	2-2	0-2

leaving dashes where the numbers representing the
effects of the new intermediate value ('1') are to go.
In this way it is clear that the two-valued matrices
are the same as three-valued matrices with the intermediate value suppressed.

We know how to fill in the gaps in the matrices

for 'p' and 'q', since these values are determined simply by the conventional ordering of the truth-table columns. But when we come to negations ('Np', 'Nq'), we find three alternatives to consider. These alternatives represent three different concepts of negation, or kinds of negation, which cannot be distinguished in the classical two-valued system. They result from the three different values that might be assigned to the negation of a proposition which is assumed to be indefinite ('1') rather than true or false ('2', '0'). Corresponding to these three alternatives, we have three different matrices for negation in three-valued logic. We can identify the different types of negation in our symbolism by writing N_0', 'N_1', or 'N_2' instead of 'N'. Thus we have

p	N_0p	N_1p	N_2p
222	000	000	000
111	000	111	222
000	222	222	222.

Since there are no established names for these different kinds of negation, we might as well give them names of our own. Let us say that 'N_0' stands for falsehood. A proposition which is indefinite is clearly not false; so its negation, conceived as falsehood, must be false (as in the second row of the matrix). Let 'N_1' stand for counter-assertion. For example, if it is neither definitely true nor definitely false that there will be a naval battle tomorrow, then the counter-assertion that there will not be a naval battle tomorrow is also indefinite. Finally, let 'N_2' stand for untruth. If the negation of a proposition is conceived as untruth, it must be true whenever the proposition itself is not true. In this sense, a proposition may be untrue without being false.

Obviously, the presence of three different types of negation will produce corresponding differences in all those truth-functions which involve negation: for example, in double negation, excluded middle, and De Morgan's Theorem. Before considering them, we should look at the other basic matrix forms.

Let us assume that a conjunction is true if both of its components are true, and false if one or more of its components are false. Hence the only question is what value to assign to it in case one component is true while the other is indefinite, or in case both are indefinite. In other words, we have:

```
Kpq

2?0
??0
000
```

Since there are three alternative values to fill each
of three blank spots, it is obvious that from a purely
formal point of view we have twenty-seven possible
matrices for conjunction. Most of these can be eliminated, however, because they are incompatible with one
another of our elementary forms of argument, upon which
the theory of truth-tables (or matrices) is based. In
the first place, we cannot fill any of the blanks with
a '2', because then we could not validly infer the
truth of each component from the truth of the conjunction itself. This eliminates nineteen possibilities.
In the second place, we cannot put different values in
the outer blanks (where p is true while q is indefinite,
or vice versa), since in that case the converse of conjunctions would not be logically equivalent. This
eliminates four more possibilities, and we are left
with the following:

```
    I     II    III   IV

   210   210   200   200
   110   100   010   000
   000   000   000   000
```

By similar reasoning, we also obtain four possible
matrices for disjunctions:

```
    I     II    III   IV

   222   222   222   222
   211   201   210   200
   210   210   200   200
```

In this sense we really have four different concepts of
conjunction, and correspondingly four different concepts
of disjunction, in three valued logic. Only the first
matrix in each case, however, preserves the validity of
De Morgan's Theorem: that the negation of a conjunction
is equivalent to the disjunction of the negations of its
components, and that the negation of a disjunction is
equivalent to the conjunction of the negations of its
components. Thus, in the first matrix for conjunction,
a zero appears where and only where either p or q, or

both, are false; and in the first matrix for disjunction, a zero appears where and only where both p and q
are false. Hence we may regard the first matrices as
representing the standard forms of conjunction and disjunction. This does not mean that the other forms are
useless, but only that we might prefer to reserve special
names for them, to avoid confusion.

In a similar way, we can argue that the second of
the three matrices for negation should be taken to represent the standard form of negation in three-valued
logic, since only this form ("counter-assertion") preserves the classical rule for double negation. Given
that we assign the values

           2
           1
           0

to any unspecified variable (p), then if the negation
(Np) has corresponding values

           0
           1
           2

the negation of the negation (NNp) will have the same
values as the original variable. Using this form of
negation also has the advantage of allowing a very
simple mechanical procedure for constructing the matrices
of negations of truth-functions and the matrices of
truth-functions of negations. Given any matrix, we can
construct the matrix for the corresponding negation
simply by replacing each '2' by '0' and each '0' by '2',
leaving the intermediate values ('1') unchanged. Given
any matrix for a two-place truth-function with antecedent 'p' and consequent 'q', we can construct the matrix
for the same function with the negation of the antecedent by simply reversing the order of the rows, or with
the negation of the consequent by reversing the order
of the columns. These transformations are illustrated
below for conjunction and disjunction.

Kpq	NKpq	KNpq	KpNq	KNpNq
210	012	000	012	000
110	112	110	011	011
000	222	210	000	012

```
Apq      NApq     ANpq     ApNq     ANpNq

222      000      210      222      012
211      011      211      112      112
210      012      222      012      222
```

Visual inspection here shows immediately that De Morgan's
Theorem is valid, because the matrix for 'NKpq' is the
same as the matrix for 'ANpNq', and the matrix for 'NApq'
is the same as the matrix for 'KNpNq'. The various
special cases of De Morgan's Theorem can be shown by
similar methods.

Now, on the analogy of two-valued logic, we might
expect the matrix for implication ('Cpq') to be the
same as the matrix for 'ANpq' (or 'NKpNq'). But the
latter matrix shows that the disjunction is indefinite
if both of its components are indefinite. This will not
work for implication, unless we are willing to give up
the classical rule of "reflexivity of implication",
that every proposition implies itself ('Cpp'). In order
to preserve that rule, we must assume that an implication is true whenever its components have the same value,
even if they are indefinite. This, together with the
assumption that an implication is true if its antecedent
is false or if its consequent is true, results in four
possible matrices for implication:

```
I        II       III      IV

210      200      210      200
221      221      220      220
222      222      222      222
```

The first of these may be regarded as representing the
standard form of implication, since it preserves the
result in two-valued logic that if an implication is
false then its antecedent is true and its consequent
false. On the other hand, it is clear that 'if p then
q' and 'either not p or q' will no longer be equivalent;
we can infer the implication from the disjunction, but
we cannot infer the disjunction from the implication,
as may be seen by comparing the matrices.

Finally, the matrix for equivalence can be constructed easily in the light of what has already been
determined, if we preserve the definition of equivalence
('E') so that

Epq = $_{Df}$ KCpqCqp.

- 175 -

In order to carry this out, we must first determine the
matrix for the converse (Cqp') of the implication.
This may be done by "rotating" the 'Cpq' matrix

```
210
221
222
```

through an imaginary third dimension on its "axis"

```
2--
-2-
--2
```

which represents the values of the function when its
components both have the same values. Hence for 'Cpq'
we get

```
222
122
012
```

Then we make use of our matrix for conjunction

```
210
110
000
```

to compute the conjunction of the two implications, or
'Epq'. This means that our resulting matrix will have
a '2' where both implications have a '2', a '0' where
either implication has a '0', and elsewhere a '1'.
Hence we obtain

```
Epq

210
121
012.
```

This result would be different, clearly, if some non-
standard form of implication or conjunction were used.

Finally, we should notice an important difference
between two-valued and three-valued logic in connection
with the notion of tautology. In two-valued logic, we
can demonstrate the validity of an inference in two
equivalent ways: we can show that the matrix (truth-
table) for the conclusion of the inference has a '1' in
every place where the matrix for the premises has a '1',
or we can show that the implication having the premises

as antecedent and the conclusion as consequent is a tautology. For example, since the two-valued matrix for 'Cpq' is

        1 0
        1 1

and the matrix for 'p' is

        1 1
        0 0,

the matrix for the conjunction ('KCpqp') of the two is

        1 0
        0 0.

Hence we can see immediately that this conjunction is true only if 'q' is true, a result which verifies the rule of modus ponens. But we can also formulate a matrix for the implication corresponding to that rule: 'CKCpqpq'. This matrix is computed by comparing the matrix for the antecedent ('KCpqp')

        1 0
        0 0

with the matrix for the consequent ('q')

        1 0
        1 0

and noting that the latter never has a '0' when the former has a '1', so that the result is a tautology:

        1 1
        1 1.

Using our three-valued matrices, however, we do not obtain "tautologies" in the form that might be expected, i.e.,

        222
        222
        222,

for every implication that represents a valid inference. Given the matrices

```
210       222
221 and  111
222       000
```

for 'Cpq' and 'p' respectively, and hence

```
210
111
000
```

for theis conjunction, we can still see that 'q' must be true if the conjunction is true. But if we compute the matrix for the corresponding implication, we get

```
222
221
222,
```

which does not seem to indicate a tautology, since the implication does not turn out to be "true" for every possible combination of the values of its components. On the other hand, it never turns out to be "false"; and in this sense it can be regarded as a kind of tautology.

Also, the classical rule of modus tollens, that we may infer the negation of the antecedent of a true implication from the negation of its consequent, is verified by our implication matrix in the sense that the value of 'p' must be 0 if the value of 'Cpq' is 2 while the value of 'q' is 0. Moreover, the same matrix shows that 'p' must be untrue (1 or 0) if 'q' is untrue. But 'p' may be untrue without being false, unless we know or assume independently that 'p' satisfies the law of excluded middle. Hence the rule of modus tollens cannot be accepted without qualification in three-valued logic.

EXERCISES

1. Using the standard form of disjunction or conjunction, construct matrices for the law of excluded middle ('ApNp') and the law of non-contradiction ('NKpNp') for each of the three types of negation (N_0, N_1, N_2).

2. Construct matrices for 'NNp', using the three types of negation in all possible ways.

3.   Show what happens to De Morgan's Theorem if the
     various non-standard forms of conjunction and dis-
     junction are used.

4.   Construct matrices for equivalence ('Epq'), using
     the standard form of conjunction but various non-
     standard forms of implication.

2.   Basic Relational Concepts

     The problems discussed in the last chapter show
that the theory of propositional forms underlying
traditional logic was unsatisfactory, and modern logical
theory has developed a new point of view based essentially on the notion of relations.

     According to the traditional view, we can take
singular propositions as the ultimate "atomic" units of
discourse from which all other sorts of propositions are
to be constructed. Quantified propositions, in particular, are to be constructed in such a way that their
truth always logically implies the truth of one or more
singular propositions. But we can see now that this
theory collapses as soon as one takes account of
propositions about empty classes. Universals of the
form 'All s are P' or 'No S are P' are true in the
event that 'S' denotes an empty class; but in that case
no singular propositions about the members of S are
true, since there are no such members. The existence
of empty classes cannot be consistently denied, since
if there were no empty classes then the class of empty
classes would be an empty class. In one sense, we can
still hold that quantified propositions are constructed
out of singulars in the modern or "Boolean" interpretation. But since no quantified proposition isolates a
specific class of individuals as its subject-matter,
no such proposition is "about" one class of individuals
rather than another; all quantified propositions have
the same subject-matter, namely the universal class as
a whole (or rather its members). Furthermore, the theory
of descriptions shows how we can reverse the classical
standpoint, if we wish, and interpret singulars as
logical constructions out of quantified propositions.
This indicates that singular and quantified propositions
are interdefinable: by way of truth-functions (implication, conjunction, etc.) we can define either type
in terms of the other.

     Hence there is no basis for the traditional assump-
tion that singular propositions have some sort of priority

or favored status as descriptions of reality. This fact becomes clearer when we realize that all of the traditional propositional forms are special cases of what may be called relational form.

In every-day language, relational form shows up in the use of transitive verbs. For example, in the sentence

John loves Mary,

the verb ('loves') is transitive because it "takes an object" ('Mary'). Naturally, we can say that the sentence is about John, the person designated by its subject term, and it assigns to him the attribute of loving Mary. But we can say equally well that the sentence is about Mary, and that it assigns to her the attribute of being such that John loves her. In order to express this alternative interpretation, we need only transform the original sentence into its equivalent passive form:

Mary is loved by John.

Each of these sentences says essentially the same thing. Yet according to traditional grammar and logic, one of them is about John while the other is about Mary, and one of them assigns the attribute of loving Mary while the other assigns the attribute of being loved by John. From this point of view, the fact that the two sentences are obviously equivalent is a mysterious coincidence. A simple way to account for the situation would be to say that a sentence of this kind really has two subjects, and that instead of merely assigning an attribute to either one of them it effectively places a relation "between" them. The two subjects are the "terms" of the relation. Clearly the order of the terms is important; for it may be true that John loves Mary, but false that Mary loves John, or vice versa. We must distinguish between a relation of John to Mary and a relation of Mary to John. Then we are in a position to see just why the mysterious equivalence holds. The passive form, '...is loved by ...', represents a relation of Mary to John if and only if the corresponding active form, '...loves...' represents a relation of John to Mary. These relations are different, but they are converses of each other. If one of them holds for any pair of terms in a certain order, then its converse holds for the same pair of terms in the reverse order. This is why any sentence formulated with a transitive verb in the active voice

can be reformulated as an equivalent sentence in the
passive voice, with the order of "subject" and "object"
reversed. Active and passive forms are understood to
express converse relations.

Truth-functional propositions - especially conjunctions, disjunctions and implications - have an
obvious relational character, although the terms involved are themselves propositions rather than persons
or objects in the ordinary sense. A conjunctive proposition asserts that both of its component propositions (antecedent and consequent) are true, in other
words, that a certain relation holds between them; a
disjunction asserts that at least one of the components
is true. In these instances, it seems to make no
difference whether we think of the relation itself or
its converse, since the outcome is the same in either
case. For implication, however, the distinction is
vital, since in general the idea that one proposition
"implies" another is not equivalent to the idea that
it "is implied by" another.

Singular propositions also have a relational
character, which is somewhat masked by the linguistic
form. If we assume that a sentence like

Fido barks

assigns an attribute (e.g., a tendency to bark) to an
individual (Fido), then by the same token it places
that individual in a certain relation to that attribute, namely the relation of "having" the attribute.
True, the attribute is not an individual object or
person like Fido, or John, or Mary; but we need not
assume that the terms in relations are necessarily
objects or persons. Or we could say that the sentence
that Fido is a member of the class of things that
bark, and again we would have a relation - class-
membership - between Fido and that class. If something possesses an attribute, then conversely that
attribute is possessed by it; if something is a
member of a class, then conversely the class has it
as a member.

Even identity-statements can be regarded as relational, although in this case the relation relates
something only to itself. We need to be able to say
things like

Hitler is different from Mussolini,

meaning that

Hitler is not the same as Mussolini,

which clearly asserts a relation of non-identity between Hitler and Mussolini. Hence we should also be
able to say that

Hitler is the same as Hitler

or

Mussolini is the same as Mussolini

and interpret these statements relationally. If non-
identity is a relation and is the complement of identity,
then identity itself must be a relation. Just as the
complement of an attribute or class is the attribute
of not having (or belonging to) that attribute or class,
so the complement of a relation is what relates terms
that fail to stand in that relation. In other words,
letting 'R' stand for any relation and 'a' and 'b' for
its terms, if

it is false that a has R to b,

then

a has non-R to b,

and vice versa.

But now, since we have just seen that singular
propositions and truth-functions are essentially
special types of relational forms, quantified propositions like those in the traditional square of opposition must also be relational forms. For we know how to
construct the quantified forms out of truth-functional
complexes of singulars. Thus all of the traditional
concepts of propositional form turn out to be special
cases of the more general concept of relational form.
This more general concept was not thoroughly explored
until very recent times.

Two general characteristics of relations have been
noted so far: (1) that every relation has a converse,
which applies to the same terms in the reverse order,
and (2) that every relation has a complement, just as
every attribute or class has a complement. We should
notice also that relations do not always have just two
terms, although most routine illustrations of them do.

Identities, for example, only have one term in the sense that identity relates things to themselves only. But many relations have more than two terms, and in principle a relation might have any number of terms. Suppose that

Fred wrote a letter to Susan;

this of course indicates a relation of Fred to Susan ('...wrote a letter to...'). But the relation itself is evidently complex, for it suggests the presence of a third term, the letter itself. Thus we could also convey the same information by saying,

A letter was written by Fred to Susan,

which looks like a relation of the letter to Susan, namely that it "...was written by Fred to..." Susan. The fact that the two sentences give essentially the same information would be a mysterious coincidence if we did not recognize that there are really three distinct terms (Fred, the letter, and Susan) involved in the relation, and that the two sentences are just alternative ways of describing this relation. Similarly, if

George's mother was married to Rachel's uncle,

we have four distinct terms: George, George's mother, Rachel, and Rachel's uncle. The proposition implicitly specifies relations between each pair of these persons (e.g., the relation between George and his mother consisting in the fact that she married Rachel's uncle). But the equivalence of these various implicit two-termed and three-termed relations can be understood only if we keep all four persons in mind as terms of the relation actually described.

The notion that a sentence might have two or more subjects, in the special sense that relations require, poses a problem. Grammatically, a sentence can have many subjects only in the sense that it can have a plural or collective subject or nominative phrase. Thus 'Horses are vertebrates' has a plural subject, and 'John and Mary are students' has a collective subject ('John and Mary'). The latter sentence may be understood as a shorthand way of saying 'John is a student, and Mary is a student', a simple conjunction of two singulars. This conjunction suggests a relation of sorts between John and Mary, namely the relation of being a fellow-student. In this case, the order of terms makes no real difference; if John is a fellow-student of Mary, then so is Mary a fellow-student of

John. If we say 'John loves Mary', however, the order is obviously important, and if we wish to think of both John and Mary as being in some sense "subjects" of the sentence then it cannot be merely as the collective 'John and Mary' or 'Mary and John'. What we need is something like 'John and Mary, in that order', or 'the relatedness of John to Mary'.

Adopting the latter alternative will give us a way of interpreting relational sentences relationally, that is, not merely as assigning an attribute to one term. Although the grammatical subject of the sentence 'John loves Mary' is 'John', presumably the name of some individual person, we may think of the sentence as being a proposition about the relatedness of John to Mary. It says, in effect:

The relatedness of John to Mary is love.

The relatedness of John to Mary, of course, is not directly indicated by any term or group of terms in the original sentence. It is indicated by what we may call the ordered pair, '(John, Mary)', of the two terms 'John' and 'Mary', where the first term of the pair is the grammatical subject of the sentence and the second term is the grammatical direct object of the transitive verb. The predicate phrase, 'is love', characterizes the relatedness of John to Mary; it represents an attribute assigned to that relatedness, or a class to which that relatedness belongs. To emphasize the class-interpretation, we substitute the phrase 'is a love-relatedness'. In either case, the phrase is constructed by transforming the original verb into some corresponding substantive (or adjectival) form representing the appropriate attribute or class.

Let us now generalize these results. Given any sentence

a R b,

where 'a' is the grammatical subject, 'R' a transitive verb and 'b' the direct object of the verb, we have three modes of interpretation. (1) We can see it in traditional fashion as a singular proposition assigning the attribute "...R b" to the individual "a". (2) We can see it in an unorthodox but equally plausible fashion as a singular proposition assigning the attribute "a R..." to the individual "b". (3) We can see it as a relational proposition assigning the attribute "R" to the relatedness "(a, b)" of "a" to "b". In this

way we obtain a propositional form which is exactly like
the traditional singular form except that its subject-
term is an ordered pair of names, not the name of a
single individual.

Since, as has been shown, we can interpret all
propositions relationally, this relational form may be
regarded as the fundamental propositional form. Hence
we need not think of the world as consisting entirely
of individuals and attributes of individuals, as the
traditional analysis seemed to require. In addition,
we have instances of relatedness and we have attributes
or classes of such instances (i.e., relations).

EXERCISES

Interpret the following sentences (a) as traditional
singular propositions and (b) as relational propositions.

1. Cicero is the same person as Tully.

2. The Taj Mahal is the Taj Mahal.

3. The Senate is a legislative body.

4. Aristotle was Plato's pupil and Alexander's
    tutor.

5. 1/2 is greater than 3/8.

3. Properties of Relations

We noted in the last section that every relation
(R) has a complement, just as every attribute or class
has a complement. The complement (non-R) of a relation
holds between all of those pairs of terms that fail to
stand in the relation (R) itself. Thus in general

Not (a R b) if and only if (a non-R b).

We noted also that every relation has a converse, which
holds from b to a just in case the relation itself
holds from a to b. Thus if we let ' ⁻R' symbolize the
converse of R, we have

a R b if and only if b ⁻R a.

This property is peculiar to relations and does not

correspond to any general property of attributes or
classes. It is expressed in ordinary language by the
use of the passive voice.

In order to define further relational properties
we must now introduce the following concepts. The
domain of a relation is the class of all those things
that bear the relation to something. For example, the
domain of the relation "...father of..." is the class
of all individuals that are fathers of someone; in
other words, it is the class of all fathers. The converse domain of a relation is the class of all those
things to which something bears the relation. Thus
the converse domain of "...father of..." is the class
of all individuals that have a father, in order words,
all offspring. The field of a relation is the "logical sum" of its domain and its converse domain: the
class of all things that either belong to its domain
or belong to its converse domain. Hence all fathers,
and all offspring, belong to the field of the relation
"...father of...".

A relation is reflexive if every member of its
field bears that relation to itself. Thus the "if...
then..." relation (or implication) is reflexive,
because every member of its field (i.e., everything that
implies or is implied) bears that relation to itself:
for every proposition "p", we know that

        If p then p.

A relation that is not reflexive is non-reflexive. For
instance, the relation "...cuts the hair of..." is non-
reflexive, because not everyone cuts his or her own
hair. The relation "...different from..." is non-
reflexive, but it is also irreflexive, since nothing is
different from itself. An irreflexive relation is a
relation such that no member of its field bears that
relation to itself. Clearly, a relation may be non-
reflexive without being irreflexive.

A relation is symmetrical if its converse also
holds whenever the relation itself does. In other
words, R is symmetrical in case it is true that

        if (a R b) then (b R a).

For example, if "a" and "b" are numbers,

        if a equals b, then b equals a,

- 186 -

so that "...equals..." is a symmetrical relation. On
the other hand, "...brother of..." is non-symmetrical,
since when A is a brother of B it does not follow that
B is a brother of A. A relation (R) such that

> if (a R b) then not (b R a)

is asymmetrical. An obvious example of this is the relation "... greater than...". Note that a relation may
be non-symmetrical without being asymmetrical.

A relation (R) such that

> if (a R b) and (b R c), then (a R c)

is said to be transitive. The relation "...less than...",
for instance, is transitive. But the relation "...next
to..." is non-transitive, because even though a is next
to b and b is next to c it may not be the case that a
is next to c. A relation such that

> if (a R b) and (b R c), then not (a R c)

is intransitive. For example, "...father of..." is
intransitive.

A relation is connected if either the relation itself or its converse relates every pair of distinct
members of its field. That is, it is connected if

> either (a R b) or (b R a)

for every pair of members ("a", "b") of its field,
assuming that

> a is different from b.

The relation "...greater than..." is connected in this
way. Given any pair of different whole numbers, one
of them must be greater than the other. But "...father
of..." is not connected. Suppose that A is the father
of both B and C; then A, B and C are all members of
the field of the relation "...father of...", but B is
not the father of C nor C of B.

EXERCISES

(a)   Describe the domain, converse domain and field of
each of the relations mentioned below. (b) Determine whether it is reflexive, symmetrical, transitive, or connected. If not, is it irreflexive,
asymmetrical, intransitive?

1.   "...larger than..."

2.   "...the same as..."

3.   "...sister of..."

4.   "...different from..."

5.   "...the author of..."

4. Similarity and Isomorphism

Relations differ from each other according to their
measure: i.e., according to how many members of the
domain bear the relation to any given member of the converse domain, and vice versa.

If not more than one member of the domain bears
the relation to any member of the converse domain, the
relation is said to be a one-to-any relation. Putting
this idea more formally: a relation (R) is one-to-any
if, for any three terms (a, b, c),

if (a R b) and (c R b) then (a = c),

assuming that "a" and "c" are in the domain of "R" and
that "b" is in the converse domain. The relation "...
father of..." is one-to-any, since every person has one
and only one father. But the relation "...sister of..."
is not one-to-any, because a person may have more than
one sister.

If any member of the domain bears the relation to
not more than one member of the converse domain, the
relation is said to be an any-to-one relation. In
other words,

if (a R b) and (a R c) then (b = c),

where "a" is in the domain and "b" and "c" are in the
converse domain of "R". The relation "...is a satellite

of..." is an any-to-one relation, if we are talking about astronomical bodies and if we assume that no such body can be a satellite of more than one other body. But the relation "...has as a satellite..." is not any-to-one, since a body may have more than one satellite.

A relation which is <u>both</u> one-to-any <u>and</u> any-to-one is a <u>one-to-one</u> relation. In monogamous cultures, for example, the relation "...husband of..." is a one-to-one relation, since there is only one husband for each wife and only one wife for each husband. For the same reasons, its converse ("...wife of...")is also a one-to-one relation; and in general the converse of a one-to-one relation is always also a one-to-one relation. On the other hand, the converse of a one-to-any relation is an any-to-one relation, and the converse of an any-to-one relation is a one-to-any relation.

One-to-one relations are extremely important in mathematics, especially in connection with the theory of numbers and the operation of counting. For if we can establish a one-to-one relation (or correlation) between the members of two classes, we can regard these two classes as <u>similar</u> in the sense that they have the same number of members; in fact, we can define what it means to "have the same number", or in other words to be arithmetically equal, in terms of this notion of similarity. For example, we know that the number of forks on a table is the same as the number of plates, if we know that there is one and only one fork immediately to the left of each plate and that no fork is immediately to the left of more than one plate, so that the relation "...immediately to the left of..." in this context is a one-to-one relation. We do not need to know how many forks (or plates) are actually present in order to know that their number is one and the same.

By mathematical induction, as shown in chapter IV (Section 4), it is possible to establish one-to-one correlations even between infinitely large classes. In this way we can show that the number of integers is equal to the number of even numbers, or the number of squares of integers; or we can show that the number of points on a line segment is equal to the number of points in a square or a cube erected on the line.

In an obvious sense, the fact that two classes are similar tells us nothing about their inner structure and is thus relatively uninteresting. But the concept of similarity, or one-to-one correspondence,

- 189 -

is useful also because it helps us to define the concept
of <u>isomorphism</u> ("having the same form"). Two classes
are isomorphic if and only if

     (a) they are similar, and

     (b) there is some relation (P) which relates
         every pair of members of the one class,
         if and only if there is some relation
         (Q) which relates every corresponding
         pair of members of the other class.

A diagram may help to clarify this idea. Let 'a_1' and
'a_2' be any pair of members of some class (A); let
'b_1' and 'b_2' be the particular pair of members of some
other class (B), correlated to a_1 and a_2 by a one-to-
one relation (R). Then the two classes are isomorphic
if and only if a_1 bears some relation (P) to a_2 just
in case b_1 bears some relation (Q) to b_2 as indicated
below:

$$
\begin{array}{ccc}
 & a_1 \xrightarrow{\;R\;} b_1 & \\
A \quad (P) & \big\downarrow \qquad \big\downarrow \;(Q) & \quad B \\
 & a_2 \xrightarrow{\;R\;} b_2 &
\end{array}
$$

    A simple illustration of these relationships is found
in the art of cartography, or map-making. The cartogra-
pher constructs a sort of two-dimensional scale-model
of certain selected features of the terrain to be represented. For example, he may draw a road-map covering
the continental United States. Then for each of the
major cities (A) in the U. S. he will locate one and
only one point or mark (B) on his map; the distance and
direction between any two cities (P) must correspond to
some distance and direction (Q) between the corresponding points on the map. Every kind of charting, graph-
ing or modelling involves the concept of isomorphism in
this way.

    But a "model" may be aural rather than visual, and
it may be imaginary or conceptual rather than real or
tangible. A printed score of a musical composition is
a sort of spatial model for a non-spatial performance,
and a good performance of the composition must be isomorphic to the score in the appropriate ways. The same
relationship holds between the printed text of a play
and a performance of the play. A representational
drawing or photograph of an object is a model of the

object as observed from a certain position, in accord-
ance with the laws of optics and projective geometry.
The uses of isomorphism in philosophy, the sciences and
the arts are indeed so numerous that one could hardly
begin to describe them or survey them adequately. In
logic, for example, we really make use of isomorphism
whenever we evaluate a particular argument in the light
of our theory of valid argument-forms. In mathematics,
we use it to establish the equivalence of different
number-systems. In experimental science, we use it in
all sorts of measurement operations: an object has a
certain length, for instance, by virtue of being isomorphic in the appropriate way to a standard measuring
instrument. In deciding legal disputes, the appeal to
precedents involves the concept of an isomorphism between the facts of the case at hand and the facts of
earlier cases. In the literary arts, isomorphism plays
a central role under the title of analogy, which is the
basis of simile and metaphor in rhetoric and poetry.
In philosophy, it plays a central role in the investigation of the problems of truth and meaning.

    Logical theory assumes that certain argument-
forms are valid, i.e., that any particular argument
having one of those forms is a valid argument. But
it does not actually specify what form any particular
argument has. In evaluating the argument

        All gems are minerals

        All diamonds are gems

        Hence, all diamonds are minerals

we "see" at once that this argument has the form of the
classical first-figure AAA categorical syllogism
("Barbara"):

        All M are P

        All S are M
        _____

        All S are P.

But the classical rule does not actually tell us how
to "see" this; it only tells us that the argument is
valid if it has that form. The argument is seen to
have that form because

        (a) there is a one-to-one correspondence

between the two sets of statements,

and

(b) the relations between pairs of state-
     ments in one set corresponds to the
     relations between pairs of statements
     in the other.

Notice that the second condition (b) is crucial, because
otherwise what functions as a premise in one set might
function as conclusion in the other, and then the evaluation would be incorrect.

Perhaps the most important manifestation of
isomorphism is in the use of analogies, which we find
constantly in every-day conversation and literature.
Their general form is:

A is to B as C is to D,

or, more explicitly,

the relation of A to B is the same as (or
similar to) the relation of C to D.

By way of analogy we can explain the meaning of what is
difficult to define explicitly, whether because of its
complexity or because of its being so primitive or
elementary that it escapes notice. Hence analogy is a
favorite device for philosophers, theologians and poets.
To suggest, for example, that God is the "soul" of the
world, is to suggest the analogy:

God is to the world as the soul of man is
to the man.

This elucidates the meaning of the term 'God', if we
assume that the meanings of the other terms ('world',
'soul', 'man') are sufficiently clear, and if we have
a sufficiently clear idea of the relation of the "soul"
to the man. Some philosophers have thought that God
should be regarded as "creator" rather than as "soul"
of the world, perhaps because they prefer to think of
the world as an inanimate object, like a machine. In
this case, the suggested analogy is:

God is to the world as the creator of a
machine is to the machine.

This analogy has the advantage over the former one that

its meaning is somewhat clearer; for we know clearly
what the relation of "creator" to "machine" is. On
the other hand, it is not obvious that the analogy is
true, since it is not obvious that the world as a
whole can be reasonably compared to a machine or
other inanimate object. One would have to suppose
that it is possible for an inaminate object to have
various organisms as parts.

Some of the most striking and influential analogies
in Western literature are found in the dialogues of
Plato, and it seems appropriate to close this discussion
with a brief examination of one of the best of these,
the analogy of the "divided line" in Republic, Book VI.*

In this dialogue, as in many others, Socrates in-
sists on a fundamental distinction between two kinds of
things, or objects of thought: sensible things, which
can be seen, heard, touched or otherwise apprehended by
the bodily "senses"; and non-sensible or intelligible
things, which can be apprehended only in thought (concepts, ideas, abstract forms). Corresponding to these
different kinds of objects, he postulates different
powers of faculties of thought: sensibility (or percep-
tion or feeling) and intelligence (rational or abstract
thinking). Then he further sub-divides the two classes
of objects, and accordingly the two classes of faculties, as follows. The sensible world consists of
"images" (sensible forms) of objects, plus the sensible
objects themselves; the intelligible world consists of
"mathematical objects" (numbers, geometrical figures),
plus "forms" (pure logical concepts).

Now Socrates suggests that if we divide a line
into two unequal parts and then divide each of these
parts again in the same ratio, the lengths of the resulting segments will represent "degrees of comparative
clearness or obscurity" among the four kinds of objects
of thought, or the measures in which they "possess truth
and reality".

Such a line might look like this:

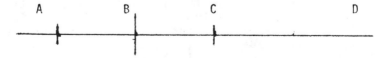

*The specific terminology in the following discussion
is given in the translation by Francis MacDonald Corn-
ford (Oxford University Press, 1945), pp. 224-26.

where the ratio of the main segments is the same as the ratio of the sub-segments within each main segment, so that

$$(A + B) / (C + D) = A / B = C / D.$$

The larger of the two main segments, C + D, stands for the intelligible world: D for the "forms", C for the "mathematicals". The other main segment, A + B, stands for the sensible world: B for the objects, A for their images. Each segment also stands for the corresponding mental power or faculty; Socrates calls these faculties 'imagining', 'belief', 'thinking' and 'knowledge' (from A to D in that order).

   The notion of "degrees of comparative clearness or obscurity" or measures of "truth and reality" is of course rather vague. But Socrates also says that the images (A) are "likenesses", "shadows" or "reflections" of sensible things (B), and he implies that the same relationship holds between mathematicals (C) and forms (D) and between the sensible world generally (A + B) and the intelligible world (C + D). So the kind of clarity, truth or reality in question is the kind that any object or concept has in relation to its various modes of representation. A picture of a tree is less "real" than the tree itself, perhaps, in the sense that it cannot adequately represent the tree as a whole but only its shape and colors as seen from a particular viewpoint. A drawing of a geometrical figure, such as a triangle, only partially represents the true properties of the triangle (since the lines are only approximately straight, have a certain thickness, and so forth). Even a mathematical object like the number two, it is suggested, is only a representation of some "form" or logical concept; but the mathematicians take such objects for granted, according to Socrates, and do not attempt to analyze them further. This rather startling thought foreshadows the modern idea of looking for the foundations of mathematics in logical theory, a project which was not and could not have been undertaken seriously until the turn of the twentieth century.

   When we meditate on the implications of this ingenious analogy, we realize that the "divided line" itself is a geometrical object, represented by the drawing we have mode of it, and presumably itself representing some deeper logical concept. One clue to its meaning, which has been generally overlooked by the commentators, lies in the geometry of the line itself. For if we solve the equations representing its proportions, as any good student of geometry in Plato's time could have done, we find that the two middle segments, B and C, are equal. In fact, the length of B (or C) is the geometric mean of the lengths A and D, as expressed in the formula

$$B^2 = AD \text{ (or } C^2 = AD).$$

Socrates never mentions these facts, and the untutored or careless reader will not notice them; he will suppose that the four subdivisions of the line have four different lengths, and he will conclude that there are four different "degrees" of clarity, truth or reality corresponding to these lengths. Thus he will be fooled by the visual appearance of the diagram and miss its true meaning, which cannot be seen by the bodily eye but only by the intellectual "eye" of logical reasoning or insight.

The fact that the segments B and C are equal shows that the corresponding objects of thought, sensible objects and mathematical objects, must have exactly the same status as to clarity, truth or reality, even though they belong to different "worlds" (the sensible world and the intelligible world). But these worlds are not quite so different as they seem. For on the one hand, the mathematical objects are merely postulated or posited as hypothetical entities whose properties can be explored by deductive reasoning; and on the other hand, the sensible objects are objects of belief, not directly apprehended by sensation (which gives only images), and their properties can only be explored by reasoning. The proper conclusion seems to be that sensible objects and mathematical objects are really the same objects apprehended in different ways. We think of an object as sensible because we have postulated it as a means of explaining the images or sensible phenomena that we experience. We think of it as mathematical because we can explore its properties and relationships to other objects by reasoning. Indeed, only a mathematical object can serve to account for phenomena. We must suppose that any sensible object has shape, size, location and motion in space, in relation to other sensible objects, so as to understand how various images or manifestations of it arise in various persons at particular times and places. Conversely, a mathematical object must also be a sensible one, or else we could find no image for it and hence no way to represent it by numerals or diagrams.

- 195 -

As the middle segments of the "divided line" are the geometric mean between the outer segments, so the world of objects is the connecting link between the world of pure logical concepts and the world of sensible phenomena. Pure logical concepts are empty forms, and they cannot be apprehended or thought except through some set of objects which exemplifies them. There is no way to contemplate a pure logical relation (such as implication, identity, class-membership, etc.) without at least imagining its terms (propositions, individuals, attributes, etc.). Pure phenomena, on the other hand, are meaningless or unintelligible by themselves; they are simply present. Without logical concepts, we could not think that one image was similar to another or different from another; we could not imagine the persistence of an image no longer present; we could not recognize it as belonging to a class of images. Thus images take on meaning and value for us only by exemplifying logical relations, and logical relations take on meaning and value by being exemplified in experience. But this notion of "exemplification" or representation is itself a relational notion, and it is really none other than the notion of analogy or isomorphism. Hence we postulate a world of sensible-mathematical objects as a way of spelling out the analogy. The object-world must be just such a world as the analogy requires. The fact that this world must be postulated and cannot be demonstrated shows that the analogy is not a perfect one. Experience refuses to be completely rationalized, and that is probably why Socrates assigns a lower "degree" of clarity to the sensible world than to the intelligible one.

But perhaps that is all to the good, since it makes life more interesting. The pursuit of understanding and wisdom is its own reward, even though the goal is never completely attained. Perfection, if it exists, must belong to the gods.